# HAPPY TO BE SINGLE

# HAPPY TO BE
## *Single*

----

## Liz
## Hodgkinson

## Thorsons
*An Imprint of* HarperCollins*Publishers*

Thorsons
An Imprint of HarperCollins*Publishers*
77 – 85 Fulham Palace Road,
Hammersmith, London W6 8JB

Published by Thorsons 1993
3 5 7 9 10 8 6 4 2

A catalogue record for this book
is available from the British Library

ISBN 0 7225 2756 X

Typeset by Harper Phototypesetters Limited
Northampton, England
Printed in Great Britain by
Hartnolls, Bodmin, Cornwall

# Contents

# Prologue

Being single is wonderful – once you get used to it!

Although it may seem strange at first to be alone, especially if you have always previously been in a family or a relationship, or have shared your life intimately with others, singleness can soon become so attractive that it would be hard to give it up for the prospect of even the most wonderful, blissful relationship.

There is, of course, the sheer luxury of being in one's own place, able to eat, relax, watch television, read books or play music without anybody in the chair opposite objecting, wanting to do something different, or wanting you to do something different.

There is the joy of having a bathroom all to yourself with no alien toothbrushes, shaving gear, toiletries, towels or flannels festooned all over the place. There is the bliss of having your very own bedroom, of being able to sleep alone, to spread yourself out in the bed, to have your sewing, reading, writing or other hobby or interest scattered over the bedspread or duvet.

There is the freedom from having to worry about waking a partner if you want to get up in the middle of the night. There is the enjoyment of being able to please yourself all the time, the pleasure of being able to have a friend round and talking into the small hours without fear of interruption. There is the opportunity to invite who you want to for a dinner party, to go out when you please and stay in when you please, to eat what and when you like.

When you're single you can, theoretically at least, have a party whenever you want to, eat out or eat in, have casual relationships, invite friends to stay. You can go on holiday where you want to and when you want to, uproot yourself if you like, all without having to consider the needs and wishes of anybody else.

When your home is your very own, you can have the decor that you personally prefer. You can create your own atmosphere, your own harmony, without the constant presence of other people who have as much right to the space as you do.

When you live alone, any dirt and disorder you create is yours alone, and for that reason, so much less annoying than the mess left by other people. And even if you are sharing a flat or house with other people, the chances are that you'll have at least some space to call your own, some privacy. As part of a couple, you may not have a single inch of space all to yourself.

Best of all, when you're single, you are not glued to anybody else in a stifling, exclusive relationship. You are your own person, able to think your own thoughts. You have space inside your head as well as all around you. When single, you can reclaim yourself for yourself, live your own life as you want to live it.

Being single can be summed up in one marvellous word: freedom.

But if being single is such an attractive option with so many opportunities for self-expression and fulfilment of individual potential, why do so few of us choose it? Why do we continue to equate happiness with having a permanent, intimate partner with whom to share your life? Why are so many of us afraid of being single, and fear that the single life is some kind of second best, when in fact it offers so much and, in reality, so much more than being part of a cosy couple?

Although more marriages are breaking up than ever before, it is still a fact that over 90 per cent of the world's population will marry at some time – and of those, the great majority will hope that their liaison will be a relatively permanent and stable one.

One of the reasons that comparatively few people have the courage to remain single is that, in our present society, singleness is seen as some kind of aberration, and the ability to form lasting relationships, preferably with a member of the opposite sex, is viewed as absolute normality, something that is a potent indicator of mental health. Indeed, Freud believed that in order to be psychologically healthy, people had to be able to become part of a permanent heterosexual couple. Those who did not wish to, or who did not seem able to, marry or enter into lasting relationships were seen as neurotic.

The impact of Freud's teachings and theories in this respect has been so great that we still tend to believe it – even though in recent years, it has increasingly come to be seen that the nuclear family is actually the cause of a great deal of neurosis.

The idea that coupledom is a sign of mental health is of comparatively recent origin. In ancient and medieval times, it was taken for granted that the single life was preferable to the married state. Indeed, the Church of England prayer book expressly states that marriage was ordained for those 'who have not the gift of continence' – as a kind of second best. The strong-minded people remained single, and devoted their lives to personal growth and spirituality. Saints have always been single, and have often been celibate as well. In the old days, remaining single and free from family or sexual attachments was considered a sign of strength, not weakness.

And even when, in Protestant countries at least, it was considered desirable for as many people as possible to marry, including the clergy, most of those unions were for economic and dynastic survival, rather than for individual happiness.

The idea that coupledom, or living with one significant other in an exclusive, monogamous relationship, can of itself confer some special kind of happiness denied those who wish to walk alone, is one that has grown up only since the beginning of the century. But it has taken a powerful hold, so much so that many people who remain single feel they have to apologize for this, or pretend that they are still waiting for Mr or Ms Right.

Part of the reason why singleness had such a bad press for the first part of this century, at least until the sexual revolution of the 1960s, was that it became part of orthodox thinking that nobody could be truly fulfilled unless they were having regular heterosexual sex. Bachelors and particularly spinsters were often considered frigid, repressed, cold, frustrated, not really fully functioning human beings at all.

And even now, when single people are most probably far more sexually active than those in a long-term monogamous relationship (where, according to all surveys, frequency of sex falls off sharply after the first couple of years), we still tend to consider there is something rather cold and withholding, somewhat selfish and aloof, something unconnected, about choosing to remain single.

The question often asked is: what's wrong with single people that they can't find a partner? Why does nobody want them? People who are permanently single are still considered not quite human, not like the rest of normal humanity who want nothing more than to mesh themselves into an eternal union with one other person.

There is the assumption nowadays that in their heart of hearts, everybody would like to find a special partner, somebody who is there for them all the time, somebody who cares, who will protect, nurture and care for them, who will provide some security and stability in an increasingly unpredictable world.

This idea may hark back to the mythical notion that at one time, humans were androgynous but somehow got split into males and females, so that we are all forever incomplete until we find our other half. It is no accident that spouses are often referred to as 'other' or 'better' halves – as if we are not whole people until we join up with another.

Present-day society is so heavily weighted in favour of couples, and so much against singles, that we are not really given a proper choice as to whether to couple up or not. The apparent choice is so loaded that it can be difficult to go against the tide. There are so many pressures put on us to form lasting, intimate relationships, and so few positive messages put out about remaining, or becoming single, that in the end, the majority of us conform. If we pair up, this means we are 'normal'. If we elect to remain single, then we are somehow odd, somehow not like other people. Few indeed are those who hold out for ever, even when they are 'natural' singles – as I suspect many of us are.

Very many people – and I include myself here – who are natural singles have felt dragooned into marrying or forming relationships when the truth is that we'd really rather be alone. So much are we told that we must find somebody, that in the end this is what we imagine we want. So strong are the pressures to couple up that it can take many years for the truth to dawn. Most of us spend so much time following paths laid down by others that we never stop to think and ask ourselves what we really, individually might want.

Then it can take years to undo the damage, to unravel the complicated web of our relationships, finances and lifestyle, and emerge triumphantly single once more.

This is not to say that everybody in the world would be happier eternally single. But because we don't have a free choice in the matter, because the dice are so loaded in favour of everlasting matrimony and pairing, it's hard to know for sure what we do want.

One of the purposes of this book is to help people discover whether they are in fact natural singles, people who would be happier untied and unattached – and to help them find the courage to untangle their relationships and emerge as people in their own right, or to accept their single state and find fulfilment as an individual.

Now that so many marriages and relationships are breaking up, many people are becoming single who perhaps have not chosen it. In America a few years ago there was an association formed for 'displaced homemakers' – middle-aged women whose husbands had walked out on them, leaving them, usually, for a younger model. These displaced homemakers were women who had never earned their own money, never had a career of their own, and they were genuinely truly stuck and adrift when their long-term relationships, which they had considered completely secure, came to grief.

These were all older women. Nowadays, around 90 per cent of divorces are brought by women, which suggests at least that very many women are desperate to become single again. (Far fewer divorced women remarry than divorced men.) Now that more women can be economically independent, and divorce lawyers often award the house, car and contents to a woman with dependent children, there is less to fear on the practical side from splitting up.

But still there is a great reluctance to face life on our own, to get out of one relationship and decide not to go into another, at least not on a permanent basis. The very thought of becoming free can be scary, in the same way a caged bird will often take ages before it dares to fly out of the cage when the door is opened. But once it is out, and has experienced the freedom and exhilaration of flying round the room, try getting it back in the cage again!

I feel that all creatures, human as well as animal, really long for freedom, but that we have become so conditioned to the cage that to spread our wings and fly out into freedom can seem nerve-racking indeed.

My own case illustrates this, and shows how our coping mechanisms and abilities to make decisions, to live our own lives, can be all too easily eroded over the years of coupledom.

Although I knew, both from the situation of an unhappy marriage in my own family, and that of many families I observed in my home town, that most marriages seemed to cause far more misery than happiness, this did not prevent me embarking, at the age of 21, on the same course.

I felt certain that my own marriage would be nothing like the unsatisfactory liaisons I had witnessed and that, unlike them, I would have a truly *modern* marriage, one of equals, a glorious companionable, harmonious relationship.

I married somebody who felt the same as I did. For many years we were married, apparently happily enough. We laughed and joked together, we both went out to work, there was no rigid division of roles, we had an equal education, came from the same kind of family background, and we were both able to earn similar amounts of money.

Most people who saw us considered that we had a good relationship. But as the years went by there was, on my part at least, a growing yearning for more privacy, more space, more solitude – a solitude that was impossible to find even in the largest house and with the kindest, most understanding partner. This yearning became ever more acute over the years, but for a long time I dared not voice it. Instead, I tried to put more 'work' and 'commitment' into the relationship. It was not that I wanted to get out of this relationship and into another, more that I longed for endless time to myself.

The longing to be alone, which I tried to suppress, finally came home to me when I was working at a popular daily newspaper. I mentioned to a male executive how very chic and smart our fashion editor always looked, how well-groomed and up to the minute. Also, I noticed how she seemed to radiate an aura of calmness and harmony wherever she went. She was a single woman who had never married and was no longer young. 'Yes,' agreed the executive, 'but she goes home alone to poached eggs on toast every night.'

To me, at the time 'having it all' and embroiled in small children, nannies, coping with a large house, dinner parties, shopping, washing and all the other myriad tasks of the modern working wife and mother, the thought of going home alone to poached eggs on toast, to a cosy tidy flat not daily devastated by small boys and their friends, sounded little short of paradise.

Now, many years later, I have just the kind of life for which I envied my fashion editor colleague – and it is wonderful, so wonderful in fact that it would be hard to give it up for anything. Or anyone.

Now that I've got used to living on my own, the thought of sharing my life and living space with anybody else is impossible to contemplate. My life now is so unmessy, so well-ordered, so unclogged by other people, that I now wonder how I coped with all those others for so many years.

The truth is, I didn't really cope all that well. I spent most of my time devising strategies for being alone. How I loved it when my husband took the boys off for a holiday, leaving me to luxuriate in aloneness. How I revelled in the few days I was able to spend alone when I managed to escape to a health farm by myself, or went off on a press trip or extended interview. I even enjoyed being in hospital to have some wisdom teeth out, as it gave me a few days' freedom from domestic responsibilities, washing, cooking, coping. And how I dreaded coming back to the mess, the fuss, the endless other people.

In my case, the craving to be alone grew and grew until it could not be contained any more – and yet I was living with people I loved, people who meant more to me than anybody else in the world. But eventually, I knew that it was actually going to be impossible to go on sharing my life with somebody else, anybody else.

And now, after several years of being single, I can still hardly believe my luck. Is my flat really all mine? Do I really never have to get somebody's dinner again, never have to contemplate a laundry basket full of somebody else's dirty washing, never have to arrange my life around somebody else's schedule and habits? Will I really always find the toothpaste just where I left it?

But although I am very positive about the single life, I can well understand from personal experience how and why so many people are reluctant to embark on it, why they make excuses to stay in relationships, however unsatisfactory they might have become over the years.

When we got married, my husband and myself were excitedly looking forward to a life of joint and individual achievements. Together, we told ourselves, we can make it. And, in a way, we did. We both established relatively successful careers for ourselves and would certainly not, I would think, be considered particularly fearful individuals. But even so, over the years of being together, 'learned helplessness' crept in, being unable to function in certain areas without relying on the other, simply through the years of intertwining.

Although we were determined not to become stuck in stifling stereotyped roles, inevitably, tasks had come to be assigned to the one seemingly most suited, or most prepared to do it. I became Queen of the Kitchen, while he was responsible for the joint credit card, the gas and electricity bills, the repairs, the car. The net result of this was that we became highly nervous of managing on our own, even though by the end we both ardently desired the separate life.

When we finally did manage to separate, we were both full of fear. I can remember the exhilarating feeling of freedom when I moved into my very own flat for the first time in my life, after more than 20 years of marriage. But at the same time it was mixed with a hideous nervousness.

I had been terrified of purchasing a property on my own. All my previous houses had been bought jointly, and with much discussion and interchanging of ideas. Now, for the first time, I had to choose a dwelling place all by myself, with nobody objective to guide or help me. How would I know whether I had bought a bargain or a pig in a poke? How would I know whether my money was safe, whether I had made a good investment? How would I decide which part of town to live in? Or should I live in a different town? Or a different country? On my own, I could live anywhere in the world. It was a heady choice – and there was nobody to consider but myself. Did I really want all this responsibility, this freedom? After all, there would be nobody to blame if it all went wrong.

It was the same when I made my other major individual purchase, a car. Again, in the past, all such decisions had been joint, made after careful consideration of the factors. However would I manage to decide on the right kind of car, all by myself? Me, a little woman who knew nothing about cars apart from how to drive them (and even this was disputed by members of my family).

Those who have never been alone, or indeed those who have always been alone, can have no idea just how terrifying all these decisions can be. Suddenly, the prop, the crutch, the life raft has gone, and you are left to walk, sink or swim on your own, having to live with the consequences of your own decisions and not having anybody else to blame if things go wrong.

Also, even though I loved those moments, days and, rarely, weeks, that I was able to steal for myself when I was part of a family, I was actually terrified of being on my own. How would I cope with all those evenings and weekends when nobody might ring? I was very nervous of having to take responsibility for all domestic decisions. What if the boiler burst? The lights fused? The flat flooded? A burglar broke in? The ceiling fell down? All these things had happened in the joint homes, and who was to say they wouldn't in my single home?

I had these fears even though I passionately wanted my freedom and single state. So I can understand how very much greater they may loom for people who have not chosen to be on their own, but have had it thrust on them by circumstances seemingly beyond their control.

But as the weeks and months of being on my own went by, I realized that most, if not all, of my fears were completely unfounded. So far, I have had no major domestic disasters, but fearing them won't stop them from happening. And every time I do cope with a blocked drain or a boiler problem, I feel that much stronger and more self-confident.

The ridiculousness of the fears we have came home to me on my first Christmas alone in my flat, when I realized that

I was actually too nervous to get a Christmas tree. Just the mere prospect of buying and erecting it filled me with the utmost trepidation.

For years, the Christmas tree had been *his* job – and what a job it was, necessitating driving many miles to a special Christmas tree plantation, choosing a prime specimen that would go from floor to ceiling in the house, strapping it to the car, driving it home, getting it into the house and putting it into a big tub filled with earth. I know it would have been simplicity itself to go to a local shop and buy a tree, but somehow – I don't know why – 'Getting the Christmas Tree' had acquired ritualistic aspects over the years.

That was bad enough, but not so bad as the ritual of the fairy lights. We were never allowed to buy new ones, and getting the old ones to work entailed them being spread out all over the carpet, us being shouted at not to tread on them, while each little light was individually tested. Eventually, triumphantly, after many arcane procedures, they lit up – and the man of the house would be warmly congratulated on his achievement.

Putting Up the Christmas Tree and Fairy Lights had been a full day's operation. Obviously, it was something quite beyond me. But when my younger son came home from university, his face fell when I informed him I would not be having a Christmas tree this year – I just couldn't be bothered. He offered to buy one from the local market and put it up. I bought new fairy lights – and the whole operation was effected in less than half an hour.

When I rang my now ex-husband to tell him, he muttered wryly: 'Curses, rumbled.' I realized that I could do it without all the fuss, perfectly well. The only mystique was that erected by my ex-husband.

But such mystique is not all one-sided. Although I soon learned to cope with my car, the boiler and the drains, I realized that I too had enacted certain rituals to make simple tasks appear more complicated and mysterious than they really were. My ex-husband admitted that he was extremely nervous of cooking, until he did a bit and realized just how easy it could be. For years he was terrified of doing pasta – 'I've just never done it' he would say – and thought he could not possibly make pastry, however hard he tried. Last year, though, he brought a batch of home made mince-pies round. 'Oh,' he said airily, 'I make pastry all the time. Nothing to it.'

It was only as each fear fell away that I realized just how greatly my coping mechanisms in many areas had been eroded by the years of coupledom. It is nothing to me to go the cinema or theatre alone these days – but for a time, I didn't see how it would be possible. Whatever would everybody think, a woman on her own? Now I realize that most people are too busy thinking about themselves to worry about anybody else. Nobody even notices I am on my own, and if they do, they are probably congratulating me for having the courage to sit there enjoying the film or play by myself, and buying my own drink in the interval.

Although I am now alone, and have no wish to yoke myself with anybody again, I am never lonely. The fears that I had about feeling lonely and unwanted, and that nobody would ring or want to see me by myself have proved as unfounded as all the others.

I would say that I have a far more active social life now than when I was married and had a constant companion always on tap. It is simply not true that women on their own are not welcome at dinner parties, certainly not true that women are not welcome by themselves in restaurants. Any restaurant is glad to have custom. It is not true that women on their own get ripped off by garages – at least, no more than men do.

People ask me: do you really travel on the underground by yourself at midnight? Do you walk down streets by yourself at night? Aren't you afraid of being mugged, raped?

My honest answer is: no, I am not afraid at all. Although it is possible that these things might happen, they haven't yet – and I'm certainly not going to let the fear of them curtail my activities. It seems to me now that the more fearless we are, the less likely terrible things are to happen. The more confident we are, the more welcome we will be at parties and restaurants, and the less likely it is that mechanics and plumbers will take advantage of us.

Being able to manage everything on one's own gives self-confidence a terrific boost, and increases personal strength and self-reliance. Now that I know I do not have to rely on anybody for anything, I can feel far more comfortable about all aspects of my life. There is so little – if anything – to be afraid of.

My overwhelming feeling about being on my own is that, finally, all the handicaps are off the horse, all the sedative effects of a long-term relationship have now receded, and that I can race ahead unhampered by other people. If I don't achieve as much as I would like, well, I've got nobody else to blame.

I believe that everybody ought at least to be able to live on his or her own, if for no other reason than that there is no guarantee of another person being always around.

In her book *The Change*, Germaine Greer makes the point that to be unwanted is also to be free, free from the demands of other people. The idea, though, that older women are 'unwanted' as partners is actually complete nonsense: there are plenty of elderly gentlemen who would like to be looked after. It seems to me that the main reason why so many middle-aged divorced and separated women never remarry or form intimate relationships is because they are far happier on their own. Fewer older than younger people want permanent partners because they prefer their own company – it's not because they become less attractive and desirable.

But the comment that because you are single you are 'unwanted' seems to be unnecessarily harsh. Just because you haven't got a partner, and have decided to remain single, it doesn't mean you can't get anybody. A lively, interesting person with stimulating conversation will always be welcome at parties and gatherings, whatever their age or appearance. And people who 'want' you, in the sense that they want to form an intimate alliance with you, may have very suspect motives indeed. 'Love' is not always what it seems – and single people can find plenty of love in their lives without having to lasso a permanent partner.

When you're single you can be truly yourself. Alone, you can get to know yourself. You can develop your talents, get to know your own strengths and weaknesses, discover both the male and female aspects of yourself.

You can become a whole person, not needing anybody else to 'complete' you. You can learn to love yourself, learn to take care of yourself, understand that you are important, not because you may be 'needed' by another, but because you are able to harness every bit of your energy for your own self-development and personal growth. It can be difficult to understand who you really are when intimately bound up with another person. It is often not noticeable how very different partners are until they split up. When together, they often seem to present a united front. But when they move into separate lives, it can be seen how very unalike they are and how, more often than not, one partner has been dominant, while the other merely followed their wishes. Until you separate, it can be hard to know how much of your life constitutes genuine togetherness, and how much is the result of one person imposing their demands on the other.

For instance, when my husband and myself were married, we both assumed that our choices in decoration had been completely joint. Together we went to choose paint, paper, furniture. But when we moved, I embarked on a ferocious re-design of my flat, while he was content to let his stay almost exactly as it was the day he moved in.

More than four years later, he has hardly moved even a chair from where it was when he took possession of the flat, with all its furniture intact. He does not have the 'home making' instinct that I seem to have, even though previously I would not have considered mine very marked.

Another couple spent many years establishing a large house full of antiques and fine paintings. It was the wife, rather than the husband, who went round antique shops and junk yards looking for bargains and just the right Victorian artefacts. Now they have separated, the ex-husband's flat remains stuffed with paintings and antiques – he has recently moved to a larger flat to house his growing collection – while his ex-wife's flat is plain and spare and sparse, furnished comfortably but extremely simply. Since her divorce, she has not been near an antique shop, and has no wish to accumulate clutter, as she now sees it, in her life.

It is often not until we can separate ourselves that we can live how we want to, in a way that is true to ourselves.

Contrary to what we may have been told, it is not selfish to want to remain single, not selfish to want to give yourself the very best and most harmonious surroundings you can find. It is, rather, selfish to inflict yourself on somebody else, to impose your needs on them, to make demands, get angry, possessive and jealous.

When you are single, you have the energy to make new friends, the energy to give to more people, when that energy is not being sapped and drained by the demands of a permanent intimate partner.

Yes, of course, there are many joys in intimate relationships. But when you are single you don't just have to have one intimate relationship – you can have lots, both with your own and the opposite sex. You can get to know other people properly, reach out to them, empathize with them, be there for them without feeling any sense of obligation or duty. There can, of course, be great pleasure in sharing things with a close friend, a lover.

But ultimately, we *are* all single and alone, however much we may try to enact rituals to deny this. No relationship, no partner, however close and loving, lasts for ever – and nor does any relationship remain the same. Like any other organic thing, it changes and grows, or shrinks and dies. If it has become frozen and stifling out of fear of looking at the outside world, it is not doing anybody any good.

In the end, you will be left alone with your thoughts, fears and emotions. Very many long-term partners are terrified of being left alone and, as they get older, express the fervent wish that they will die first, so terrified are they of facing life on their own.

Ultimately, there is nobody who can be guaranteed to help us allay our fears, stop us from being frustrated, miserable or depressed, or take away the pain of living. Nobody else can live our lives for us.

The reality is that we are alone. So why not make the most of it, embrace it, go with it, choose it? It doesn't mean we will have to be lonely – far from it. To be able to be single means that you have grown up, that you have shed a childlike dependency on others.

The truth is that there is only illusory security in relationships. Any can end at any moment, abruptly and without warning, however together the couple seemed, however grand the wedding, however intertwined the lives. The only real strength and security comes from the ability to be alone.

It is enjoyable and rewarding to be able to be alone. It is fun. It increases self-confidence and self-esteem.

No, you don't *have* to be single, any more than you have to be in a partnership. I have experienced both, and can say that however ecstatic, however close a relationship might be, however great the rapport, reliance on another person is ultimately weakening.

If you are single, intend to be, or are wondering about the single life, you can congratulate yourself. You have taken the important first step on the road to self-realization and lack of attachment. And paradoxically, once you free yourself from the stifling need to become closely attached to one other person, you can attach yourself far more closely to humanity in general.

You can become *more* warm, *more* loving, more empathic and a more valuable person, both to yourself and others when you are able to extricate yourself from the mesh of intimate exclusive attachments and begin to operate in the wider world.

# 1
# Why Aren't More of Us
# Single?

*A*ccording to the latest statistics, around 95 per cent of us are, have been or will be married. That's a higher percentage than at any other time in history. At the same time, as is well known and often lamented, ever more people are getting out of marriages and long-term relationships. The monogamous one-partner-for-life idea has been replaced by a constant merry-go-round of relationships where people keep marrying or setting up house with each other. All this constant change of partners means that there are, as well as more marriages than ever before, more single people than at any other time.

But, as is all too evident from the proliferation of singles clubs, dating agencies and lonely hearts ads, many of these single people are just living in limbo, hoping that the person of their dreams will magically materialize, so that they can become doubles once more.

The idea given is that singledom is a temporary and unsatisfactory state of affairs which will be ended just as soon as the right person happens along. Even among those who are part of a couple, many men and women feel that all they have to do is to ditch the boring tedious spouse – and find true, lasting happiness with some wonderful new person who is out there.

We are given to believe that in the real world, there are hundreds and thousands, maybe millions, of marvellous people we can date.

But when first, second, or even third and subsequent marriages and relationships so plainly aren't working for an ever-larger number of people, perhaps we should stop and ask ourselves why it is that so many of us are desperate to hitch ourselves more or less permanently to one other person. Why are so many of us still hoping to find that one special love in our lives?

The important question is: are these intimate liaisons we all seem so desperately to want socially constructed, merely an aspect of our present society – or is there a deep, abiding, biological and emotional urge to want to attach ourselves to one other important person?

Many radical feminists consider that women do not and have not had a proper choice in the matter. They believe that in our overwhelmingly male-dominated society, women are pressurized and conditioned into 'heteroreality'. This means that most women grow up believing that in order to be complete, to be fulfilled, you have to find a suitable man, as early as possible, and settle down with him. Otherwise, you risk being 'left on the shelf', or becoming a 'frustrated spinster'. But if there were a genuine choice, they say, if singleness were presented as the norm rather than an aberration, far more women – and men, of course – would choose to remain unattached.

In her book *The Spinster and Her Enemies*, British academic Sheila Jeffreys, who describes herself as a 'revolutionary lesbian feminist', says that until very recently, there simply has not been, for women at least, a viable alternative to the 'sex slavery' of marriage. Most women in the past, she says, simply had to form lasting ties with men, just in order to survive. It was not possible for most of them to earn their own livings as they were denied proper education, and they were not allowed to fulfil any role other than that of wife and mother. The monogamy of these women, Jeffreys suggests, was socially constructed, as was the desire for motherhood.

Motherhood, which most women can achieve without effort, was elevated into something almost mystical, to make women happy with their chains, content with constant childbearing, or the threat of this. And as there seemed no alternative, no other way of living one's life, the sensible solution was to make a virtue out of a necessity, to sing the praises of the married life, and to make the single life seem dreary and confined by contrast.

Because they have not in fact freely chosen the roles of wife and mother, Jeffreys believes many women feel they have to validate it. They have to make out they have chosen their lot, otherwise they could not live with themselves. It is always extremely painful to admit that you may not have made a choice of your own free will, but the choices for women within a patriarchy are limited indeed.

The other way of justifying the lack of choice available was to maintain that it was 'natural' for women to be secondary and to want to have children above anything else. Few women like to be called 'unnatural', and so most conformed, with only a very few courageous spirits holding out.

Many men have claimed that all their creativity, their achievements in the world, have been but as a poor substitute for the ultimate creativity in women of being able to give life. But as we all know, any creature, even an amoeba, can reproduce its own kind – there's nothing very special about that. Also, in most cases, the vaunted 'creativity' of women in being able to bear children has, through the ages, most often not been freely chosen or within their own control. It's something which has just happened, and which has ruined their health, taken away their chances of being free and independent, and has made them completely dependent on men. That is the reality of women's wonderful 'creativity' in being able to give life.

American feminist Mary Daly believes that mothers propel their daughters into marriage, or lasting liaisons, because they want to validate what they themselves have done. If their daughters follow joyfully in their footsteps, they won't feel they've made such a mess of their lives after all, whereas if they supported their daughters in their struggle to find independence, autonomy and a successful career, it might reflect too painful a picture of their own lives. It seems to be human nature to want everybody else to be in the same boat we are in ourselves, to drag other people down to our level. Think how often alcoholics try to press drinks on people, how often gamblers urge others to have a little flutter. If others do what you have done, this somehow makes it all right.

'Where there is very little alternative and the choices are loaded,' Sheila Jeffreys writes, 'any other choice becomes a difficult struggle.' Even nowadays, that struggle is not over.

Women still feel they have to justify not being attached to a male. It's as if it's something second rate they have settled for, rather than chosen as being superior to that of glueing themselves to somebody else.

In a recent interview, the broadcaster Sue McGregor, who stated that she was probably 'one of nature's singles', still felt she had to justify her 'unusual' decision to remain forever unmarried by saying she could not have combined her career with marriage and children, and that now she 'slightly regrets' not having had children.

What a different world it would be if women felt they had to justify being married, had to justify attaching themselves to a male, and bringing yet more unnecessary people into the world! Then the choices might become altogether different, and those who remained single would not feel they had to apologize for their non-attached status.

The feelings of having to justify remaining single is not confined to women. Bachelor singer Cliff Richard is always being asked in interviews whether he 'regrets' not having a wife and children. He always says no – and recently has taken to adding that he feels many people secretly envy him his single status.

He keeps saying that he is perfectly happy being single. But do those interviewers, who are usually themselves bound into relationships which they are certain they have freely chosen, really believe it? Most people believe that if we remain single it is simply because, for one reason or another, we have not yet found the right person, and that if we did we would be perfectly happy to bind ourselves to that person and become a stereotyped couple. If we succumb in the end, that validates what so many others have done.

But I don't want to become an alcoholic just so that it makes you feel happier with yourself being an alcoholic.

But if the radical feminists are right, and many women marry and have children because they are not rewarded for doing anything else in our patriarchal society, why do so many men want to get married and have children, too? Is there some similar social construct limiting their free choices?

Psychologist Heather Formaini, author of *Men: The Darker Continent*, says that many – if not most – men feel at a certain time in their lives that they ought to get married. So they look around for a suitable victim, marry her, and then imagine that side of their life is taken care of – they don't have to give it any further thought.

It's not so much that they deeply want to get married, or that they have fallen desperately in love; more that at a certain stage in their lives, they want to have the complete kit – they want to appear normal. Having got their careers off the ground, they now want to play the 'husband and father' role. Even if they don't really want to, they feel they *ought* to want to, and eventually this becomes the same thing.

Heather Formaini writes:

*Many men do say . . . that they didn't marry for love but to establish a household, and sense of order in their lives. As Chris [an interviewee] says, opportunism plays a major role: when a man feels that convention demands marriage, he will look around and find a woman to marry. Whereas women see love and marriage going hand in hand, men tend to see marriage as a social adjunct – a state that will be advantageous to them as they move through their lives: it bolsters their status, their job, their political life, whatever they are involved in. It gives them a good background from which to operate, no matter what social group men come from.*

At the core of this need to marry, Formaini continues, is a neurotic need to remain locked in the mother's arms, but not so enclosed that escape is not sometimes possible. A man may marry and divorce several times, she says, and never see that he is repeating a pattern that is longing to be ended:

*He does not see that his infantile psychology is pressing him to confront the nature of his humanity and move into a new psychological state which will give him the option truly to be human.*

So, according to Heather Formaini, men as well as women feel that marriage is something they have to do in order to look right, to enact the rituals of our present society. But it is precisely because so many men marry simply in order to establish a household, to look right, and because they do not love the women they marry, that large numbers of women quickly become disillusioned with marriage, or at least that particular marriage, and divorce the husband if they possibly can. Even so, the hope that somewhere, somehow, a wonderful relationship with one other person might happen, perhaps with a 'new man' or a younger man, never quite vanishes.

Nowadays, of course, women can divorce with more confidence than ever before, because they can earn their own livings. The sheer number of divorces these days –

approaching one in two marriages in many Western countries – cannot be separated from women's new ability to be economically independent. In the past, women did not dare to divorce men – at least, not unless these men could provide lasting alimony for them, and very few men would be in that position. Also, divorcees were social outcasts until the 1960s, considered to be, in some sense, 'scarlet women' – or women that 'respectable' married ladies would shun.

These days there are fewer economic reasons why people should want to marry – and yet we're still doing it. Can social constructs, and men feeling that it's about time they 'settled down', really be the only reasons why so many of us want to become part of a couple?

It seems to me there is more to it than that – and in order to get at least part of the answer, we can look at the situation of gay and lesbian people. Here, there are not the usual reasons for wanting to form an intimate liaison. Most gay partners do not expect to be kept; by forming a permanent liaison with a member of the same sex, they are setting up a household which is not sanctioned by society, and they certainly do not want a partner for the look of the thing, to add status and make them look normal. If anything, setting up a gay household makes them seem abnormal to the majority, and prey to homophobia.

Gay relationships afford no legal protection or improvement in status. In fact, none of the usual reasons for wanting to marry (apart from having a regular sex partner) apply to homosexual people. So why are so many of them keen to form relationships?

Could their longing for loving intimate relationships mean that there is something other than society's conditioning at work, some deep longing in all of us to have a special person in our lives? After all, there is very little encouragement in our present society to become gay.

The gay actor Sir Ian McKellen has said that in spite of conditioning into heterosexuality from every sphere during his formative years, he still became gay. One lesbian friend of mine, who has been in the same close relationship with another woman for more than 15 years, told me that she had been brought up in a typical middle-class English suburb, where girls were expected to take a secretarial course, join the local tennis club and the Young Conservatives, and hoped to get an engagement ring on their finger by their eighteenth birthday. My friend had never even heard of lesbianism, and certainly did not know any gay women. And yet, in her case, even the most ferocious conditioning was not enough to make her conform.

The fact that homosexual people form close one-to-one relationships may indicate a deep longing to bond with another, over and above social pressures. And in almost every society since earliest times, men and women have formed couples, and there have been marriage ceremonies of one sort or another. Although marriage itself has gone through many changes over the centuries, and the dynastic or economic marriage has given way, largely and increasingly, to the 'companionate' marriage, one more of equals, the fact that most people couple has remained a constant.

Some psychologists believe that all of us, even the most apparently self-sufficient and secure, have dependency needs and that we are social animals who are not basically meant to be on our own. There is the feeling that human beings have a powerful attraction towards each other, something which goes beyond conditioning or social constructs, male domination, or even largely emotional, unconscious needs such as wanting security, love and companionship. It is something programmed deep within us, to want intimate contact with other people.

There is also the question of the sex drive. So how much is this a powerful reason for wanting close exclusive relationships? Again, there are widely differing views on how much the sex drive is something innate, and how much a matter of conditioning, upbringing or expectations. In the past, many people seemed to manage perfectly well without apparently expressing any 'sexuality' at all. Now, we are considered hardly human unless this side of our natures is given regular, orgasmic expression.

The late Bhagwan Shree Rajneesh, who founded the famous 'sex ashram' in Poona in the 1970s, believed that sex was a natural urge for women as well as men, but that marriage, monogamy and bearing children were not. Pregnancy, he said, was a torture to many women, and something that most would like to avoid.

By contrast, Sheila Jeffreys believes that for women, heterosexual intercourse is little more than a highly successful method of continuing male supremacy and domination. Our so-called sexual freedom, by which is meant the freedom to have ever more sex, came in only when more and more women were managing to escape marriage, she says. Some way had to be found to bring all these 'spare' women back to male domination – and sexual intercourse was the means by which this would be achieved.

Although in the past most women did not enjoy sexual intercourse, and considered it a grim duty which they dare not refuse in case their husbands turned them out, in the twentieth century ideas changed so radically that it was to become not only enjoyable but something you had to do in order not to be 'repressed' or 'frustrated'.

'During the 1920s', Jeffreys writes, 'there was a massive campaign by sexologists to conscript women into marriage and motherhood and compulsory intercourse. The eroticizing of the married woman, previously seen as sexless, became an important task, and sex was seen to be the pivot of the relationship.'

Sex, Jeffreys now considers, plays a vastly inflated role in heterosexual relationships, and women who refuse to comply are seen as frigid and unnatural. Yet, she says, male domination would be overthrown at a stroke if women were allowed to voice their natural distaste for sexual intercourse.

Women's 'frigidity', she says, made men feel uncomfortable for perpetually imposing themselves on women, and so they had to blame the women for not responding. Female frigidity, Jeffreys considers, is a potent form of resistance to male domination.

But it wouldn't do to have too many women escaping from male domination, so a major campaign was instigated at the beginning of the century to make sex central to everybody's life. Previously, large numbers of both men and women seemed to have managed perfectly well without it. In Victorian times, all academics had to be celibate (or at least, unmarried) and very many professional and religious men seemed able to contain their sexual drives without too much trouble. There is little evidence either that single women, in the days of Jane Austen, George Eliot or the Brontës, for example, were greatly troubled by being unable to satisfy their sex drives.

Now, of course, all is different. It is an assumption nowadays that we all have more or less insatiable sex drives which can be 'satisfied' only by the continuous presence of an intimate partner. Most women's magazines have at least one article on how to have a good relationship, how to get and keep your man or how to enjoy sex, in every issue. The idea that young women could be sexually rampant was unknown until the 1960s, when Helen Gurley Brown, American editor in chief of *Cosmopolitan* wrote her bestseller, *Sex and the Single Girl*.

And now a spate of men's magazines – new, serious ones rather than the top-shelf variety – carry articles on exactly the same thing – how to get and keep the girl of your dreams.

It is difficult, maybe impossible, to say how far sex is an innate drive and how far a social construct. Certainly, all animals indulge in sexual activity, and we see this as part of their fundamental animal nature. But animals have no choice but to obey their instincts if they possibly can. The main thing that separates humans from animals is that we have a choice, we have brains and minds which can weigh up possible consequences of our actions.

When we are young, there is certainly great curiosity about sex. Partly this is engendered by all we read about sex these days, or see on the screen – it is unlikely that young people in the past would have given quite so much thought to this activity. But the fact is that young men get erections very readily. It is also a fact that young women are attracted to young men: males are by no means always the instigators of adolescent sexual activity. It seems unlikely that heterosexual sex is *merely* a social construct, something which subdues women into secondary roles, although, of course, it does have this effect.

Freud, as we know, believed that sex was a primary urge and that although we might repress or sublimate it, it remained the prime mover for very many of our actions. I believe the truth is not so much that sexual intercourse is the primary urge, but that as incomplete and vulnerable human beings, we have a great 'urge to merge', to get close to other people, when we do not feel strong enough to manage on our own. Sex hits us at times when we feel especially vulnerable, and it is a mixture of curiosity, a longing for closeness, a physical urge and a desire to alter our consciousness. It can act very much like a drug, and the very real disease of sex addiction is now becoming recognized.

But it seems to me that there is more to the desperate urge of so many of us to form relationships than the look of the thing, than social conditioning, or even expression of the sex drive. At the heart of our compulsion to enter into relationships, and the way we feel bereft when we are not in one, is that fact that so many of us feel lost and incomplete on our own.

In the past, life was more stable and there were more support systems. Now, as people are increasingly alienated from their families, they move to strange towns, new countries, and move next door to people they don't know and may not ever get to know, the need to cling on to other people, to be 'in love', becomes greater than ever. And as we can't rely on anything very much any more, we feel that at least we ought to be able to have a strong, stable relationship with somebody else.

So we seek this out, elevating it in importance above personal growth and fulfilment. As life becomes ever more fragmented and uncertain, the feeling that we must join on to another person becomes ever more acute.

I do not want to compare the past over-favourably with the present and imply that everything in the past was all right, while everything in the present is horrific. But the fact is that, in many ways, life was very much more ordered and stable, and there was consequently less of an urgent need to become a couple at the very first opportunity. In the days of the extended family, when everybody in the neighbourhood knew everybody else, most people had their allotted place in life. There would be a place for the spinster aunt, the unmarried uncle, the brother or sister who stayed at home to look after father and mother. There would be family and friends around.

One only has to read Victorian novels to see how little most people were alone in those days. Young people did not live in flats, and most stayed at home until they were married. If they went to college, they lived in college rooms, again in close proximity to other people. The orphan child Jane Eyre was an odd and unhappy phenomenon.

Now, of course, there are very many only children, single-parent families, people living by themselves in strange towns, people who do not know a single soul in the place where they live. This could never have happened in any time other than our own.

Also, today, many of us feel increasingly alienated from our families of origin. In the past, most people simply followed what their parents did, without thinking too much about it. Indeed, there were very few alternative ways of life open to them. Aristocrats followed the set pattern of their lives, and peasants and artisans followed theirs. There was little choice, little mobility in life, little opportunity to move away and establish a separate, individual lifestyle, particularly for women. Women of all classes were kept at home, even when the men ventured out into the world. With such narrow horizons, and the only role models available those of parents and forebears, we just naturally followed their examples.

But then came the great impact of education, travel, psychology, and the discovery of the importance of unconscious motives. It is no accident that psychology and psychoanalysis became popular at exactly the same time as society as we had previously known it became fragmented for ever, with the old limited ways of life forever shattered. The old order changed – but we had no real strategies for establishing viable new methods of behaviour. Naturally, we clung to what we knew – getting married, having children – at the same time as wanting something different, something better for ourselves.

One of the most important of the ten commandments is that to honour our father and our mother. This can be seen as a dangerous doctrine indeed, leading us to repeat their mistakes and dysfunctions in case, by doing something different, we should attempt to criticize and not honour them. So we have repeated abuse, alcoholism, gambling, codependency (a term of American origin, denoting those who are able to gain a sense of self only through their relationship to others, who over-depend on others and need to be needed), and other unsatisfactory forms of behaviour because we have wanted to validate what our parents did, wanting to believe that they knew best and did what was best.

Now, of course, we have been given permission to look closely at our parents' behaviour and lifestyle and find it all very severely wanting – a blueprint for how not to live our own lives. We have been given permission to 'divorce' our parents, to act differently from them. This is all very well, but it means we have to find something more satisfactory for ourselves. And this can lead us to feeling even more alone and lost. We can't in all honesty accept our parents' values – but where do we find better ones of our own?

All this discomfort can so easily lead us to seek solace and refuge in intimate relationships. But, more often than not, these couplings are born out of yearnings and feelings of inadequacy than anything more positive.

When we feel lost and lonely, it is only natural that we should yearn to connect with other people. But for most of us, the only way we know how to connect is by repeating the behavioural patterns we have observed, even when these do not serve us very well. American psychologists Robin Norwood and Susan Forward have drawn attention to the way in which very many people, especially women, are drawn into unsatisfactory, dangerous or violent relationships because of low self-confidence and self-esteem.

People who come from abusive or alcoholic backgrounds seek out abusers or alcoholics, simply because this seems known and familiar to them. They then, without really realizing it, repeat the patterns they have learned, and so it goes on. We form relationships to try and fill up the emptiness in ourselves – and this, I believe, happens over and above whatever social pressures may be exerted, stro.. though these undoubtedly are.

But the sad truth is that nobody at all can fill up what is empty inside ourselves – and this is why so many relationships are doomed to failure, even those which apparently survive. Whenever we try to connect with other people out of a deep feeling of need and inadequacy inside ourselves, we will never be able to have a good relationship.

Psychologist Susan Jeffers says that relationships based on need are like applying sticking plaster to a wound. They can never be fulfilling for very long. When people make early relationships and early marriages they are very often, perhaps usually, dependent, lonely, frightened people. Because we are not basically connected to our own essential selves, we try to reach out and connect to somebody else. In our ignorance, we assume the very reason we feel so lost and alone is because we do not have a truly fulfilling and satisfying relationship with somebody else. If we had, we tell ourselves, all our problems would be solved. 'But without primal connection with ourselves, true connection with others is impossible,' Susan Jeffers writes.

She sees the prime motivation for latching on to other people as a feeling of unrelenting loneliness and emptiness within ourselves. We form intimate relationships to try and fill this sense of loneliness within. If you ask people why they contact dating agencies and write out lonely hearts ads, they will overwhelmingly tell you it's because they are lonely. Of course, it can never work, because one lonely person just attracts another lonely soul – and the loneliness is compounded.

You may not feel it so acutely because there is always

somebody there. But such relationships hardly ever work for long, simply because one inadequate, lonely person is hardly going to satisfy another such for very long.

With hindsight, I can see that this is what happened to my former husband and myself. We were both young, both in a strange town where we knew nobody, and we were both cut off, by education and aspirations, from our families of origin. We did not have anybody to turn to – so who else did we choose but somebody equally young, vulnerable, lost and alone, someone with whom we seemed to have much in common? We thought, in our ignorance, that we could give each other the strength we individually lacked. We saw each other as a life raft, forgetting that rafts do not help you to learn to swim.

Intimate relationships, and those which have, over the years, contracted into partnerships where habit and indolence have replaced early intimacy and passion, all too often constitute a kind of anaesthetic, a sedative which works to stop us from getting to know ourselves, or facing the reality of ourselves. For so many of us, there is the underlying feeling that if we did have a chance to get to know ourselves properly, we might not like what we found. So we stick to forming relationships where we can look outside ourselves, and blame the other person when things go wrong.

Marriage can, and usually does in our society, constitute a kind of displacement activity, where you can become so busy coping with the other people in your life that you never give yourself time to discover who you really are. The more children you have, the more relationships you enter into, the more sex you have with a greater variety of partners, the more alienated from yourself you risk becoming.

Those women who, in the Eighties, were supposed to 'have it all' were, in reality, bustling about with a hundred and one displacement activities, all of which made them look very busy and important, but each of which also stopped them from getting to know who they really were, and what they really wanted out of life.

The question is: how do we start, instead, to form relationships out of love and trust and through healthy functioning? For the point of being single, or being able to be single, is not to go and live in a cave as a hermit and cut yourself off from the rest of humanity, but rather to have a greater sense of empathy and connectedness to everybody around you.

When enmeshed in passionate, intimate relationships and families, the danger is that we not only don't get to know ourselves, we don't get to know anybody else properly either. We are so busy trying to fulfil other people's needs, and cram in all the jobs and tasks we have set ourselves, that we never allow ourselves any time whatever for peace and quiet. We have little time for friends, or to cultivate genuine relationships based on close but detached rapport.

In the past, many of us needed to form relationships in order to survive economically. Peasants needed each other to help run the house, livestock and land, while the aristocracy needed each other to preserve their dynasties and families. Nowadays, the fact is that in modern Western societies, we simply don't need each other in order to survive ourselves. True, nobody can be completely self-sufficient, but it's perfectly possible to go through life without binding a single person to us. We can get jobs and homes and live our lives without having to rope anybody else in.

But even though we no longer need to, we still bind others to us. We have come to see intimate relationships, regular sexual activity, as signs of emotional health. Yet we are more dissatisfied, disorientated and yearning than at any other time in history. We seek beautiful relationships – but on the whole, we do not find them.

I believe that we can never, ever find happiness inside relationships. We fall in love, we become passionate, when we do not love ourselves, when we feel so ill at ease with ourselves that we can hardly bear to be on our own. We fall in love at times of major life change, when life is in limbo, when we are vulnerable. It is at these times that we most long to connect with somebody – and the chances are that when we feel the need to fall in love, we will soon find somebody to fit the bill.

But the more we can learn to love ourselves, the more we can learn to fill up that yawning emptiness inside without attaching ourselves in permanent ways to others, the less will be our need to have other people constantly saying: 'I love you' – and then demonstrating that love by buying us cars, jewellery or other consumer durables.

In place of this need can come self-confidence, a new attractiveness, and a capacity for friendship and non-attached but close relationships, which are all the more satisfying because they are not formed out of fear and self-loathing. When we can remove within ourselves reliance on others, we can start to fulfil our own potential and walk through life alone but not lonely.

It is hard to have a close, intimate human relationship

which is not ultimately dysfunctional – unless we take the steps to understand the dynamics which propel us into these relationships, and keep us tied into them long after they give us any joy or pleasure.

Yes, of course we need to connect to other people. But when we remove that fearful need to connect to one other especially significant person, we can then connect properly both to ourselves and the rest of humanity.

It is only when we feel strong and resilient within ourselves that we can have good relationships with others. For many of us, this will mean staying, or becoming, single, or overhauling the existing relationship to such an extent that it changes out of all recognition – and you need to be in complete harmony with the other person to be able to do this. Theoretically, I suppose it might be possible to establish 'singleness' and space within a relationship, if this is what you both want. The problem is that all too often, the other person in the partnership wants to continue exactly as before.

The reason why more of us don't remain single from choice is mainly because we are nervous and afraid and we don't want to seem all that different from other people. We are nervous of doing what most people don't do, we are afraid of facing the world on our own, we feel lonely and lost and we don't like ourselves very much. The danger is, if we continue in relationships which do not help us to grow, that we never will find ourselves, never reach our true potential as human beings.

You owe it to yourself to be able to be single. When you can enjoy your own company, when you like being alone, and when you have the confidence to contact friends and arrange joint activities without waiting for somebody else to

*47*

do it all the time, when you can quite happily go on holiday, stay in hotels by yourself and go to restaurants and cinemas by yourself, then you have truly grown up.

If you have to have somebody by your side all the time, then you risk being stuck in an adolescent mentality which prevents you from discovering all aspects of yourself. So many people never really discover their true selves, understand their genuine likes and dislikes, until they can be alone for a bit.

It is in solitude that one's true self becomes apparent, that potential can be fulfilled, genuine creativity expressed. In the next chapter we will take a look at the positive side of solitude – so often seen as a kind of punishment, something that few people would freely choose.

# 2
# The Bliss of Solitude

*A*lthough for many of us relationships constitute the most exciting and dramatic events of our lives, and although humans are above all social animals, the fact is that most, if not all, worthwhile creative endeavours are accomplished alone, when people are by themselves.

In fact, it seems to be solitude, rather than company, that sets the creative process in motion. Most works of genius are the inspiration of a single mind at work, rather than collaboration, or even 'inspiration' by another.

Teamwork and co-operation are important, of course, but behind every successful (and even unsuccessful) business venture, behind every work of art, behind every empire, is the inspiration of a single individual. Those who wish to create a work of art, who want to grow spiritually, or accomplish some great and unusual feat, need time alone to think – it is in silence and quiet thought that the mind works best.

However much we may want to cling to relationships, the fact is that nobody else can think our thoughts for us, nobody else can pass our exams for us, feel our emotions for us, take away our pain, or live our lives for us. We are all unique individuals with an individual destiny, and true, authentic development of the self is possible only in solitude. It is only when you are alone that you can get to know yourself, discover your true talents and potential.

In his book *Solitude* – one of the few modern works to talk positively about being alone – psychiatrist Anthony Storr reminds us that most great philosophers have been essentially solitary people. Gibbon, author of *The Decline and Fall of the Roman Empire*, said that conversation enriched the understanding, but that solitude was the school of genius.

The current wisdom, says Storr, assumes that humans are social animals who more than anything else crave companionship and affection. Yet the paradox is that many of the greatest thinkers of all time have never had families, or formed close personal ties with other people. He adds that the idea that we need constant companionship from the cradle to the grave, and that if we want to be alone this means we are somehow odd, started only in Freud's time, as did the notion that solitary people are unhappy or unstable people who cannot form close relationships. According to current orthodox thinking, one of the main ways of assessing a person's mental and emotional stability is by whether they are able to form close and lasting ties with other human beings. If so, then this is an indication of their social health.

In fact, Freud went so far as to state that mental health is possible only when people are able to form intimate, lasting heterosexual relationships. We tend to imagine nowadays that satisfying human relationships are our only, or at least, our chief source of satisfaction and happiness, but Anthony Storr puts forward the possibility that it is much more likely that interests, hobbies and personal achievements provide a far greater source of happiness – and on the whole, these can be done only when one is alone.

For most of this century, Storr says, creative endeavour has been viewed as a poor substitute for living relationships, a kind of second-best activity. But as the century ends, we are slowly coming back to the idea that it is most probably the relationship that is the poor substitute, the anaesthetic, the sedative.

Recent work on addiction, codependency and dysfunctional relationships have shown that the ability to have a lasting relationship with just one other person, to be monogamous, faithful and to remain married, is no indication whatever of emotional health. There are many people who absolutely have to be in a relationship, who cling to that relationship long after it is dead, and who are often controlling, clinging, fearful, emotionally blackmailing individuals, attaching themselves to others in a needy way.

These are the people who dare not be alone, who cannot stand the thought of their own company for very long – because they have very little sense of self-identity. Those people who are happy to be by themselves, who can make decisions on their own, take responsibility for their own lives, are now increasingly being seen as the truly healthy ones.

Of course, there are great differences between being able to be alone, and being a loner – somebody who is actually unable to reach out and form satisfactory relationships with other people. Loners are those who never seem to fit in anywhere, who are alone because nobody much likes their company, or because they are simply unable to relate to other people, to have empathy with them.

Undoubtedly, some of Anthony Storr's great male philosophers would have fallen into this category. But the kind of solitude I am talking about, the sort that is blissful, is the *ability* to be on one one's own, not the *inability* to form relationships and ties with other people. The truly happy single person is one who reaches out to others, who has close friendships with many people, but who does not rely on anybody, depend on anybody, have expectations, or make demands on others.

All learning requires solitude, as does the completion of any important piece of work. It is when we are alone that insights come and negativities can be dispelled. When we are constantly with other people, never spending a moment on our own, it can be difficult to get to know who we are, what we want, what is our destiny.

But when we cut ourselves off from other people for a time, our imaginations can get to work and our creative potential begin to be fulfilled. Although there is a great yearning these days for satisfying relationships – supposing such an ideal could be achieved – there is also an ever-growing number of people going on retreats for holidays. There is so little opportunity these days for most people to be alone and quiet, we have to go to special places to achieve silence and solitude.

Although nobody would recommend solitary confinement as a way of life, it is a fact that very many authors have begun their best work while in prison, when they have had plenty of time to think, undisturbed by the ordinary processes of living. One of the most famous examples is that of John Bunyan, who wrote *Pilgrim's Progress* when in Bedford jail.

A period of aloneness puts you back in touch with yourself. For genuinely creative people, says Anthony Storr, achievements are of far more importance than their personal lives. Very many great people have spent large chunks of their lives alone, or at least, not in intimate attachments to other people. After the Crimean War, Florence Nightingale went to bed for 50 years with some mysterious illness so that she could escape the demands of her family, think about the future of nursing and write books on the subject. Jesus retreated into the wilderness for forty days and nights to be alone to think.

Many religious people, writes Anthony Storr, might argue that encouraging people to look for their own fulfilment in a relationship with somebody else has done more harm than good. And certainly, anybody who really wants to follow a spiritual path has to do so alone. 'Particular friendships' are discouraged in convents and monasteries, and those who are serious about their spiritual growth are usually advised to cut off intimate ties with other people.

Most great thinkers of the past and present have understood that when we form intimate, exclusive attachments with others we are cut off from important aspects of personal growth. Although we can learn a lot about ourselves through our interactions with other people, it is only when we are alone with ourselves that we can truly discover who we are, and what we want – as distinct from what others might want for us.

One trouble, of course, with close intimate relationships is that they are always liable to end, and in any case, the likelihood of two different people being able to see eye to eye for year after year is extremely remote. What happens, more often than not, is that the more submissive partner's wishes are subsumed into what the more dominant one wants – so two people are not living full lives realizing their own individual potential.

This can be seen in the lives of many male artists and composers, who have been given the silence and peace necessary to get on with their work, while their wives wrap their entire lives around the great man. The result is that when the great genius dies, the wives are left bereft and with no sense of identity. For them, it has been a wasted life, although I know many people would defend what they did as their choice.

While Augustus John was painting, and getting commissions, his first wife Ida Nettleship and his second wife Dorelia McNeill were having babies and looking after the great man. Neither woman ever achieved any individual recognition and there was no thought given to the possibility that they too might want to paint. By contrast, Augustus' sister Gwen, increasingly being recognized as a greater artist than her brother, withdrew into ever-deeper solitude in order to have plenty of time to develop her art. It would not have been possible for Gwen to paint as she did if she had been surrounded by endless children and a demanding husband. She realized this, and after her relationship with Rodin ended, she hardly saw other people at all. Perhaps this is not a life that most women, or indeed most people, would choose, but Gwen decided to dedicate her life to her art.

The result is that although her art is of very narrow dimensions, in that she painted the same subjects over and over again, she is now recognized as one of the greatest woman artists of the century. Such dedication is rare – because it is still not encouraged in women – but it makes us realize that women are just as capable of great art as men, so long as they become 'selfish' enough to pursue it.

It may be that great creativity, true genius, is given only to a few individuals. But that doesn't mean that the rest of us shouldn't have a chance to do what we can while we are here, and not waste our lives with the demands of others. In order to be truly creative, for each one of us to maximize our own individuality and creativity, it is necessary to be able to bridge the gap between external and internal reality, to make connections between the two. For this, we need periods of solitude.

It is probably true to say that many more people would find genuine creative potential within themselves if there were more importance given in our present world to the advantages of solitude. Being alone, says Anthony Storr, can exercise a healing function by enabling us to get in touch with ourselves, and developing our true interests.

In our present society, many of us fear being alone. We are afraid of our own company, because we are afraid of the thoughts that tend to arise. For this reason, a lot of people are terrified of meditation, because they find unwelcome, nasty thoughts come into their head, rather than the peace and bliss they have been told they should be experiencing.

The reason why horrible thoughts tend to come up during periods of meditation, increasingly recommended as a way of relaxing and calming oneself after over-stressful experiences, is because we never give ourselves a genuine chance to get rid of them. We try to drown nasty thoughts, or stop them from ever rising to the surface with drink, noise, sex and constant companionship, but there will still, inevitably, be times when we are alone and they threaten to rise up. The thing is not to be afraid of them, but to go with them, let them come to the surface and try to understand why they arise and what they are trying to tell you. Otherwise, they never go away, but deepen our fears of being alone.

The ability to be alone is a potent sign that you have grown up. Babies hate to be alone for any length of time, and become terrified if they are left for more than a few hours. To them, it seems as if they have been abandoned for ever. Small children also become frightened if left alone, when they are in the dark, and when there is no comforting adult around. As we grow up, we become 'best friends' with our contemporaries, and as we grow up still more, although not completely, we tend to fall in love and want to form intimate attachments to other people, maybe for life – or at least, that's what we tell ourselves.

Yet all this is a sign of emotional immaturity which is why, as people get older, they tend to place less and less insistence on the importance of intimate personal attachments. They begin to be able to manage perfectly well without them; so well, in fact, that the thought of having another person invading their life permanently is not attractive any more.

When I was a university student, I believed the worst thing in the world would be to have to live in a flat or bedsitter by myself. I could not imagine how I could stand such a life, although I knew many students did live alone. I felt sorry for them, not having any close friends with whom to share and considered them the unfortunate lonely people. They were, on the whole, alone not because they particularly enjoyed being alone, but because they did not know how to reach out to other people and be friendly.

Now, the greatest luxury I can imagine is to have my very own space. The more time we are able to spend on our own, the more we learn to come to terms with solitude, and how not to drain our energies trying to cope with and please other people. Realizing that you can actually enjoy being alone is a major discovery for very many people. Most of us simply do not give ourselves the chance to discover how marvellous it can be to have periods of uninterrupted silence, to go to bed alone and sleep alone in a clean comfortable bed.

I know that I have gained many strengths since being alone, strengths that would have been impossible when I was in an intimate relationship. I've got to know myself better, and I like myself better as well. I have been able to heal past wounds, and to inject a sense of personal purpose into my life, which was difficult when others were making incessant demands.

Also, importantly, I have gained many more friendships than would have been possible glued together with somebody else. Living with another person makes you lazy about forming friendships.

In the past, men have often had the chance to be alone, and this has been respected. Men who work at home very often have their own study, and their right to peace and silence is respected. What is often not appreciated, or has not been until very recently, is that women are human beings too, and can also become more creative, more whole, more complete people when they can spend times entirely alone.

Bhagwan Shree Rajneesh reckoned that very few women in the history of the world have ever become enlightened because on the whole, they have never been able to have time for themselves. 'They live, they produce children and they die,' he said in one of his sermons. Women have been expected to bustle around and look after others, denying any needs of their own. He said that 'a woman is not only capable of giving birth to children, she is capable of giving birth to herself'. This birth is possible only when there can be solitude. The myth of 'having it all' contained this fatal flaw – there was never any time to be alone. Bustling about and being eternally busy can be as potent a sedative as anything else we have discussed, and all sedatives and drugs work in the same way – they separate you from yourself. It is for this reason that mind-altering drugs and substances are not allowed in most serious religious paths.

In all religions, according to Bhagwan, women have not been accepted as candidates for the ultimate growth of consciousness, and one of the main reasons for this is that they are never allowed to be alone, never allowed to be by themselves. In India it has been accepted for centuries that once a man has finished being a householder, finished bringing up a family, he is perfectly entitled to go off into the wilderness to seek his own personal growth and enlightenment. It is accepted that in order to do this, a man must be able to be on his own, free from the constraints of other people. Few women, in the past at any rate, have ever been able to enjoy 'the bliss of solitude.'

But now that, at last, we can have it, it seems to me we ought to be able to take advantage of it. As ever more women extricate themselves from unhappy and unsatisfactory marriages, they are realizing that they can please themselves – and it is a heady realization.

One major reason why women in the past have not been able to enjoy the bliss of solitude is because they have been burdened with children. As most women who have ever had custody of small children for any length of time will know, there is no loneliness on earth to compare with that of being with small children. Almost all women I know who have had children, and been cooped up with them, long for solitude. You simply can't have it when children are small, however much help you may employ, because they are too demanding – and it's difficult to have it as they get older, as they take up so much space and are so noisy.

The humorous columnist Dulcie Domum (really writer Sue Limb), who chronicles domestic mayhem weekly in *The Guardian*, is always imagining, trying to achieve or actually achieving a few hours of blissful solitude, away from the children and Spouse. Bhagwan states in his book *A New View of Women's Liberation* that the presence of a family will always hinder personal growth. (I am not a follower of Bhagwan, but consider that in spite of all the corruption that happened around him, he did at one time offer genuine words of wisdom.) There has never been, he says, any instance of anybody having a family after they became enlightened, and there never will be, because families are the most effective ways of preventing personal growth, the most absolute hindrance there is.

True equality of the sexes, it seems to me, will come about only when men and women enjoy equal freedom to be alone, to be silent, and when this choice is respected.

How do we know the difference between solitude and loneliness? It's not always easy, and for those who spend time alone, there will inevitably be periods of feeling lonely, when there are great acres of silence and space that you would like to be filled up with another person.

Susan Jeffers says in her book *Dare to Connect* that we should never be afraid of loneliness, because it can lead us to greater exploration of who we truly are and what we have to offer to the world. Many of the ceaseless activities into which we plunge ourselves are attempts to blot out loneliness, so we do not have to face it. When we are able to face it and understand that there is nothing whatever to fear from it, we can welcome being alone and enjoy the solitude.

It is important to realize the difference, though, between blissful solitude and the kind of aloneness which is painful and depressing. Solitude is bliss when you are never afraid of anybody leaving you, when you feel strong enough to cope on your own if necessary, and when you feel autonomous, independent and complete in yourself.

Lovers, especially at the start of a relationship, are always uneasy, always fearful that their partner might want to end the relationship, or might die, meet somebody else, fall out of love. And so, through their fearfulness, they try to bind the other with presents, with rings, legal documents, emotional blackmail. But still they have no feeling of security. Only someone who is capable of being alone, said Bhagwan, is truly capable of being a friend – because they do not need you. The true friend enjoys your company, but does not depend on it, or pine if it is not available.

All intimate relationships eventually increase anguish and misery. It is only when we can stand alone that we can actually have good friendships and genuine rapport with other people. But the more time we spend alone, the less likely we are to want to form intimate attachment – there is simply too much to lose. We lose our own space, for instance, including the important space inside one's own head, when it is taken up with the restless demands of other people.

Also, according to Bhagwan:

*Once you accept your aloneness, your emptiness, it becomes the opposite – an overflowing of energy and joy. Don't have faith in anyone.*

Ultimately, the only person you can rely on is yourself. Welcome periods of solitude, and if they get too much, remember that you can always do something about it. You can always phone a friend and arrange to meet. When you become used to being alone, you gain the confidence to do this, to renew old acquaintances and to suggest meetings, outings, activities. Nobody is suggesting that you spend the rest of your life in solitary confinement.

In her book *A Passion for Friends*, American feminist Janice Raymond extols the virtues of friendship over passionate, exclusive attachments. She points out that to be alone is not to be lonely, but gives the chance for 'companionship with oneself'.

'Thinking is where I keep myself company,' she writes. 'Where I find my original friend. Thinking is where I am at home with myself, withdraw from the world.'

It is only through thinking that it is possible to discover one's true self. Time alone to think is particularly important for women, Raymond believes, because until you can be a friend to yourself, it is difficult to reach out and empathize with other women. And it is not possible to be a friend to others until you are a friend to yourself.

True friendship, Raymond feels, is closely tied with the ability and freedom to think. Many great philosophers of the past put enormous value on human friendships, and they also realized that friendship was impossible without enough time to be alone and think. Few women have ever had this luxury, but those who have, those who realized the importance of periods of solitude, have been the best friends to other women.

Virginia Woolf realized the importance of having a circle of women friends, and also the need for a 'room of one's own' in order to develop creativity. She made sure she lived her own life and was not at the beck and call of others. She developed a great capacity for friendship, a capacity which, Janice Raymond reminds us, was denied her sister Vanessa, the painter, because so much of Vanessa's time was taken up with her family and their incessant demands.

It is in periods of solitude that we can develop self-confidence, self-esteem. Janice Raymond believes that because most women have not, until very recently, had a chance to be alone and think, and have been given to understand that their major role in life is to minister to other people, they have not been self-confident and self-aware and have certainly not been particularly friendly towards other women. Those women who have wrested time for themselves have often done so in the face of enormous opposition, and have risked being called unnatural and unwomanly.

Periods of solitude are not necessary only to remain in good emotional health. They are also essential for maintenance of physical health. It has been known for some time that one of the best ways to recuperate from a serious illness is to be able to spend some time alone, to be quiet and relaxed. When the demands of other people become too incessant, the system risks being overloaded, so that exhaustion follows.

The controversial British cardiologist Dr Peter Nixon believes that the most recuperative thing humans under undue stress can do is to be quiet, relaxed and away from other people – for a time, at least. As it can be extremely difficult for busy, hurrying people to wind down, he will sometimes admit them to hospital just so that they can be rested under medical supervision. Often, this is the first time such patients will have been alone for many years. And it is in this period of aloneness and quiet, removed from all distractions, that healing often takes place so that heart bypass or transplant operations are no longer necessary. Given periods of peace and quiet, the body can often right itself without recourse to surgery or strong drugs, he believes.

Dr Nixon is convinced that the main problem in society today is 'hurry sickness', where we feel we must constantly rush about and cater to the demands of other people. Such restlessness, he considers, is a major cause of many, if not most, of our serious modern chronic illnesses.

In the old days, it was understood that all humans needed periods of quiet and contemplation in order to recharge the batteries. Unfortunately, nowadays, it is becoming ever more difficult to wrest times of quiet for ourselves. Dr William Dement, who pioneered the scientific study of sleep in America, believes that our modern life is not conducive to having the sleep we need for proper rest and recuperation.

He says that because of the telephone, the fax machine, jet travel, television, videos and other modern distractions, nowadays people sleep less than at any other time in history. As a result, we are becoming a world of chronically exhausted individuals.

A book that became very popular in the 1970s, and helped to underline the belief that in order to remain well, everybody should have an intimate marriage-type relationship, was James Lynch's *The Broken Heart: The Medical Consequences of Loneliness*.

The author, an American professor of psychology, said that human interactions can profoundly affect the physical workings of the heart. Loneliness, he says, caused by widowhood, marriage breakup or the increasing isolation of life in big cities, has brought about great social fragmentation which has resulted in internal organs malfunctioning.

He maintains that there is a biological basis for establishing close, intimate relationships, and writes: 'We must either learn to live together or increase our chances of prematurely dying alone.' To back up his case, Lynch cites examples of 50-year old women dying of cancer not long after their marriages have broken up.

The book's main thrust seems to want to tie us down to permanent marriages: 'Marital status is one of the best predictors of health', he writes, and cites studies to show that married people experience a lower mortality rate from all causes than single people – married people are more likely to survive serious illness, rather than die prematurely. Single and divorced people remain in hospital far longer than married ones, he says.

He adds that chronic health conditions are far more likely to affect those who live alone. Blood chemistry, adds Lynch, is significantly changed by human companionship. Very few people want to be lonely and most want to find love, he states. But the fact is that many people who do live alone will have tried and failed to develop satisfactory human relationships.

Lynch has a point, of course: unrelieved loneliness eats away at the soul. But the mistake he makes is to equate loving human relationships with marriage, or other bonded type of partnership, and to imagine that one has to choose either between being married, or being forever alone and lonely.

He writes:

*Great value is now placed on independence, individualism and new found freedom, but far less value is placed on dependency. To need somebody else is seen as a sign of social weakness, a sin . . . It is becoming increasingly difficult to share the most basic human truth – that we are really dependent on each other. Saying we are self-sufficient means that we are deceiving ourselves. Our mass media suggests that it's good to become independent of other humans.*

Lynch seems to believe that all human problems connected with loneliness can be solved by finding the 'right person'. This dangerous doctrine can trap us all into permanent relationships whether we want them or not – simply because we are so afraid of the idea of being lonely, and of not having anybody in our lives who cares about us.

What Lynch misses is that the reason lonely people are

lonely is because they want to take, not give. The solitary person who does not actually *need* other people, but who can still reach out to them, invite them to dinner, phone up friends, arrange meetings and outings, may be alone, but he or she will never be lonely. Nobody who is capable of reaching out to others and establishing rapport will find themselves lonely.

Lonely people are those who have never learned to enjoy their own company, not simply those who are single or divorced.

Unless we can come to understand the value of periods of solitude, we will not learn to value ourselves. We are here to fulfil our own destinies, not those of the people around us. It is only through solitude that we can learn the real value of human relationships, which is to be close and companionable, but to be able to stand alone, detached and separate from others.

The trouble is, it is increasingly difficult to stand alone in a world full of people, bustle and hurry. We are told again and again, until we are in danger of believing it, that we are not fully human unless we have an intimate relationship of our own, something permanent and one-to-one.

It is actually the greatest lie of the century. I'm not saying, of course, that everybody wants to go through life alone, and it can certainly be extremely comforting to have people who care about us around at times of vulnerability and strain. It is only comforting, though, when there is no over-reliance on either side, when these people do not rely on you or depend on you, and you do not feel that everything would immediately fall apart if they left.

I said at the beginning of this chapter that relationships, particularly when they involve falling headily in love, are often the most exciting phases and incidents in an ordinary person's life. They are the instances of 'high drama' that everybody can have.

But the feeling of being alive and charged with super energy that often comes when relationships are new, is illusory more often than not, just another drug that separates us from our true selves – and also from genuine connection with other people.

Writers Susan Curtis and Romy Fraser say in their book *Natural Healing for Women*:

> *Many women and men feel at their most connected and powerful when they fall in love. The outpouring of energy towards another person leads to an experience of love filling our lives. It seems like a profound spiritual experience, but what we actually do is to project all of our energy and emotion onto another person who has become an object of our desire. When that initial stage of infatuation passes, we return to whatever state we were in before and do not learn to build any lasting qualities as a result.*

Those who can learn to enjoy being alone are the happiest and most fulfilled of people. When we desperately want to attach ourselves to other people, we are out of touch with our true natures. When we can enjoy being alone, we can experience both the bliss of solitude and the joy of never feeling lonely.

The two go together.

# 3
# The Single Life –
# By Single People

*S*o far, we have been speaking theoretically of the many advantages of being single. But what is the reality like for those who chose to be single from the moment they realized they had a choice, for those who became single after many years of marriage, or for those whose spouses or partners suddenly left them? And what about people who have gone into relationships after very many years of being single? How do the two compare?

## Sister Jayanti

Jayanti, an Indian woman in her early forties, decided at the age of 14 that she would always be single, even though a marriage had been arranged for her by her traditional Hindu parents when she was one year old. She is now director of the UK branches of the Brahma Kumaris Spiritual University, a worldwide organization dedicated to the furthering of world peace by encouraging individuals to make important changes to their consciousness. One of the mottoes of the University is 'when we change, the world changes'.

Although born in India, Jayanti was brought up and educated in London, attending a girls' grammar school and London University before deciding to dedicate her life to a spiritual path.

Today, she lives in a house with several other female members of the Brahma Kumaris – all the directors and administrative heads of the Organization are female – and spends her time travelling round the world giving lectures, seminars and talks. It is a life which, she says, would be completely impossible if she had to look after a family.

She says: 'When I was about 14, I had to make a choice between arts and sciences. Although my natural bent was towards the arts, I chose science as I felt it would be easier to have a career, and keep my independence.

'I chose medicine because by so doing I could remain single and keep my respectability. Medicine is always a respected choice for Indian children, male or female. Somehow, deep in my soul there was a yearning for independence, even though this was firmly discouraged in my society.

'There is, even nowadays, little opportunity for an Indian woman to be independent. Even her passport has her father's or husband's name on it.'

There was, she says, considerable opposition to her choice from her extended family, even though her father was willing to allow her to have the educational opportunities she needed to become a doctor.

'I wanted my life to be one of service,' she says. 'Then I came into contact with the Spiritual University, and realized that physical medical aid was limited, and that the same energy could be channelled into my own spiritual development – something which, I thought, would not be possible if I had a husband and children.'

The point is, says Jayanti, that even if you share a room with somebody, you have to give some time to that person, out of common courtesy. 'If you are married, and raising a family, you have hardly any time to yourself. And as the whole upbringing of Indian women is to be tolerant of whatever their husbands do, and to treat them almost as gods, the opportunity for personal growth hardly exists at all.'

She adds: 'In modern relationships, people believe they can fulfil each other's needs. Yet this becomes an area of conflict as the years go by, and great disappointment sets in. I do believe, though, that the urge to find a partner is something that is very deep within us, and that if you don't have any spiritual knowledge you can easily believe that the way to find happiness is through an intense relationship with another human being.'

Jayanti believes the single life can be hard unless there is a supportive community, a close circle of friends. Although community life might seem to hold all the answers for those who want to be single but are afraid of loneliness, she points out that this life too has its dangers and drawbacks.

'As with a marriage, there is some surrender of independence,' she says. 'There has to be a lot of give and take. The difference is that in a community, whether this is a religious or a secular one, everybody is striving for the same goal, everybody wants to make it work. There is not the same distraction of time and energy when everybody wants the same things.

'A community can be a tremendous support, but you have to have the right attitude and also plenty of self-respect, because if you need specific support, you may not get it.'

Present-day relationships, Jayanti believes, go wrong because there are such high expectations. 'There is a feeling nowadays that we are not whole people on our own, that we need somebody else to "complete" us. But when the intellect is bound up with the needs and wishes of other people, there are too many distractions to be able to follow one's own path properly.

'It is a fact that to achieve any great work, whether this is a work of art or following a spiritual tradition in order to grow personally, one has to be single-minded. Anybody who wants to achieve has to go it alone – there is simply no other way.

'In order to achieve anything worthwhile, you need all the energy you can muster, and the more human beings you have around you, the more this energy is likely to be dissipated and distracted. One major difference between living in a community and in a nuclear family is that with the community, there are specific jobs assigned to individuals.

'For example, we have drivers, cooks and people who work the computers and technology. In a nuclear family, by contrast, very often the woman has to do everything – earn money as well as do all the domestic chores. Very few people are able to satisfy the needs of the family and also those of the wider world – we have to choose.

'My own choice was that I did not want to be restricted to domestic chores and bringing up children. I have never wanted children, and now see it as a service to humanity that I, at least, have not reproduced.

'Women often believe that through motherhood they are going to fulfil themselves, but this is a mistaken belief. There is never any way of fulfilling oneself through catering to the needs of others.

'In a community, one has a wider circle of friends but there is no particular attachment to any one person. Of course, one has more rapport with some people than with others, but nobody is intimately bound up with another.

'As I see it, it is only through having the courage to be single that women can find their true selves. It has always been recognized that you have to be single to follow a meaningful religious path. One reason for this, apart from the fact that energies are not depleted in caring for a few other people, is that when you are single you can realize both the masculine and feminine aspects of yourself and not hand them over to the significant other in your life.

'When you are single, you are forced into playing both roles, and this is no bad thing. It's very tempting when you have a partner to leave a lot of the decisions and day-to-day management up to them, to shed some of the tasks. When you're single you can't do this.

'I believe that being, or remaining, single can make you a far more valuable human being than when you are tied up in an intimate relationship. At the very least, you have learned to look after yourself and not be a burden to somebody else.

'Plus there is the fact that however secure the relationship might seem, there is always the possibility that you can be stranded at any minute, unable to cope. There is never any guarantee that any relationship will last beyond today.'

# Julie

Julie, 24, has decided that she will never marry or have children. She graduated two years ago from Oxford University and after spending a year in America, is about to embark on an MA course in visual anthropology. She admits she doesn't know what she wants to do as a career.

She says: 'Although I seem young, I've absolutely made up my mind. I can see my friends getting engaged and married already, and it horrifies me.

'I think what has put me off is the experience of my mother. She was quite a high-flying career woman until she married and had children. She gave up her career to follow my Dad in his job, and then the marriage fell apart. Instead of becoming independent, as she could have done, she married somebody else with the result that at the age of 50, she has no job and no money of her own. She is completely tied, with no idea whatever how she would earn her own living.

'I did come perilously close to getting married when I had an affair with a man more than 20 years older than me. He had never been married before, and felt he'd like to have a go at it. I was very much in love with him, and it would have been extremely easy to say yes.

'But the affair ended, quite acrimoniously and bitterly, after a year. At least it was relatively easy to leave him, and establish a new life for myself. Think how difficult it would have been if we'd been married – and possibly had a baby. That experience decided me once and for all. When I met him, I thought I would be in love with him for ever.

'But as time went by, his irritating side began to show, and

I also felt that I needed the company of people my own age. I'm now going out with somebody a year younger, and it feels much healthier.

'Although I don't yet know exactly what kind of career I want for myself, whether this will be some kind of writing or lecturing, or something quite different, I know that marriage will make it all more difficult, not easier. I would hate that feeling of being trapped, of having to be responsible for somebody, and coming home to the same person night after night.

'I had that experience when I was living with my older lover – and know that it's not for me as a lifetime's decision. The trouble is, it's so easy to get sucked into trying to make a relationship permanent when your own life is in limbo. When I left university, there was a horrible feeling of being adrift.

'I feel that I have now got over that. I've established myself as a proper grown up, independent person, and I've passed the serious danger point. My feeling of relief for not tying myself down when I had that intense relationship is so overwhelming that it taught me a very valuable lesson about myself.

'When you don't know yourself it's so easy to lose yourself in a relationship, imagine this is what you want, when all the time it may not be. I don't know how long my current relationship will last, but with this one there's no sense of tying myself down, and we certainly won't be setting up house together, or anything like that.'

# Margaret

Margaret, 45, was married for 20 years and has been single for four. She has no children, and is currently taking a full-time art course. Margaret has had a varied career, training initially as a biologist, then moving into advertising and PR. She also, in later life, trained as an actress and followed this profession for several years.

With her former husband, Margaret has travelled all over the world. They are still good friends, and see each other regularly, although there are no plans to get back together again. Neither has a current partner.

She now lives in a small three-bedroom cottage which pulses with harmony and comfort. Books line the walls, there is a Steinway piano, and classical music is played constantly. One of the bedrooms has been turned into an artist's studio and there is a potent atmosphere of achievement and purpose.

Margaret says: 'If I could sum up my single state in one word it would be: freedom. Not just the freedom to come and go as I like, but the freedom to have my own space, which cannot ever be invaded by anybody else without my express permission. When I was married, my husband was always diving into my handbag – and couldn't appreciate why it should upset me.

'I feel in our society that women particularly are not given proper choices as to how to conduct their lives. When we got married, I was just 21 and my husband and myself were completely equal – we were both at university, and we graduated with the same degree.

'But before long, the imbalance began to be felt. I had just started an MA course in a Northern university when my husband started to apply for jobs in London. He was accepted for one, which meant my coming down with him – I never really considered staying to finish the course on my own.

'But then it was downhill all the way. He became the big earner, while I fitted in my career with what he wanted to do. I felt in those days it didn't matter who earned the money – something I have radically changed my ideas on since. I know now that earning money is extremely important in our society, because it gives power.

'Gradually, as the disparity between our earnings became ever greater, my self-confidence plummeted to the point where, in company, I didn't even dare to offer an opinion on anything. I had no self-esteem, and no idea how to climb back up. In the meantime, our relationship got worse and worse.

'I kept thinking there was something wrong with me. Then my husband started his own company, and spent more and more time abroad – and this gave me time to think. I secretly started going to a women's consciousness-raising group, and the scales began to fall from my eyes.

'I realized that the choices I had made meant that I was no longer a whole human being. I had compromised and sacrificed so much, believing that my role was to be supportive. Then a series of accidents and disasters happened, which made me seriously question my whole lifestyle.

'Our beautiful house, which I had spent years redecorating and refurbishing, caught fire – and in a single evening, all my work was destroyed. It took a year out of my life to get the house habitable again. I then sustained a serious back injury. All the time, our relationship was getting terrible. I moved into a separate room, and locked the door at night – just to get some privacy.

'I went for marriage guidance, tried to patch the relationship up, but in the end, I realized I had to leave, for my own sanity.'

Margaret says now that she does not blame her husband – she went along with what he wanted to do without being sufficiently assertive – but has 'reclaimed' herself since becoming single.

'In the end I had to ask myself: if I left my husband and got nothing at all, would I still want to leave? When the answer came out yes, loud and clear, I knew I had to do it.

'I was absolutely terrified. I had never been on my own, never been a single person as an adult, had never lived by myself. But it's been wonderful. I did everything very methodically, getting my finances sorted out, deciding where I wanted to live, and what I needed for my own personal growth, and to make myself aware that I was an intelligent, thinking woman.'

Margaret did the Alexander Technique, went for aromatherapy sessions, travelled, took up the piano, joined Mensa and made a new set of friends. 'I began to realize that many of my former friends, mainly married women, were not supportive, and I had to find a new circle of friends who would support me in what I was doing.

'I realize now that you do pay a price for going against society's norms, and people still think it's odd that I should actually enjoy living alone. But I've learned to enjoy my own company, to care for myself as an individual and to give myself the diet, amount of sleep, exercise and social life that suits me best. It was very important for me, when I divorced, to get a new bed – not a single one or a double one, but a three-quarter size which gave me enough space without having marital connotations.

'I would say that sleeping alone is one of the greatest benefits of all of being single. I sleep so much better and now could not bear the idea of having somebody climb in beside me every night. It's also an enormous relief to me to be free of somebody else's sexual demands.'

Has she ever been lonely, or felt that a ready-made social life was lacking? 'No! I've been invited to *more* dinner parties, more social functions and been out more in the past four years than in the twenty before them. I now often go to the theatre, which is a great love, whereas for 20 years I hardly went, as my husband kept falling asleep.

'People have told me that I look ten years younger since becoming single. For me, married life meant a great deal of stress and very many compromises. I've had to learn to be more assertive, and this has been a hard lesson. I have a tendency to defer to other people, and this of course did not stand me in good stead in my married life, as my husband was extremely assertive and ambitious. I sort of got lost along the way.

'Whether I would have been like this with somebody else, of course I can't say. But now it seems that I am a natural single and at the moment I do not envisage a long-term relationship. It may happen, but at the moment it seems unlikely.

'Something that has come home to me since separating is how very different in every way my former husband and myself were. Other people considered we had a good relationship, at least for much of the time, but now I realize that a lot of this was PR, how we wanted to present ourselves to the world.

'I think it took me such a long time to get round to separating because my own parents had divorced, and divorce seemed such a failure to me. But I don't have any regrets. I'm just glad that at long last I'm doing what I want to, pleasing myself and enjoying myself.'

# Paul

Paul, 50, was a single man until he was 32, when he married Jenny. Ten years later he was divorced, and has been single since. He has a teenage son, is not currently in a relationship and does not expect to marry again. He lives in London and is a teacher in a large school.

Paul says: 'I was quite happy being single until I was about 30, when all my friends seemed to be getting married. Suddenly, I felt lonely. Jenny, a colleague in the school where I then taught, fell desperately in love with me and I suppose I felt sorry for her. I also felt that it was time I got married and settled down.

'Looking back, I realize that what married life gave me simply wasn't what I wanted. Jenny was extremely competent, she continued to work full time, she looked after me very well, and it was thanks to her that we bought our first house. I had been quite happy living in rented accommodation, and I liked the idea of impermanence, that I could up and go without having to sell or have too many ties.

'During the years I was married, I tried to settle down into being a standard husband and father. But the roles simply didn't suit me. I loved my son so much when he was born and was overcome with tenderness. But gradually, life began to narrow down.

'Jenny became unhappy with living in London, and wanted to move to the country. She felt it would be a better environment for our son. I went along with this, and soon I lost all my bachelor friends. When I was single, I had a large circle of friends, male and female, and I used to enjoy meeting up with them, exchanging ideas and having social evenings.

'These all disappeared until in the end we had no friends at all. My marriage became a kind of displacement activity, which stopped me looking at myself and asking what I really wanted. It wasn't until Jenny said she wanted a divorce – we'd been having terrible rows – that I realized freedom was what I wanted after all.

'I felt terribly bitter, rejected and angry – and it took me a few years, I would say, to come to terms with the fact that she no longer loved me. But I never loved her. I felt sorry for her, and also lonely at being the only single man around, as it seemed. Yet I would never have left her.

'She has given me my freedom and although I have found it hard to adapt to being single again, it is the ideal life for me. My only big regret is the effect it's had on our son, now 14. He comes to see me most weekends, and we get on well. Yet the relationship has become artificial, and I don't feel I have a continuous input as regards his education and future. He comes to see me one Saturday, he has a problem and we discuss it. But the next week, it's something else, and there is no follow through.

'Also, Jenny and I don't really present a united front. Although she has been extremely careful not to run me down in front of him, I know she really does not want to have anything to do with me. It's still making me feel bitter that we can't be friends, can't discuss things like sane adults, and we still have rows, usually over things to do with our son.

'I've considered going away and letting our son lose contact, but we do get on well, and I know how he looks forward to coming to London to see me, especially now he's a teenager, and London seems exciting to him.'

Paul adds that if he has any real regrets, it is that he ever got married and became a father in the first place. 'Of course, it's ridiculous to have regrets, but I can't help thinking that if Antony did not exist, I wouldn't have to have anything whatever to do with Jenny, and nothing would please me more.

'I realize now that I am not really husband and father material. I like to feel free, to follow my own desires, to give up work and take a course, or go round the world if I want to. She was always going on at me for not earning enough money to enable her to give up her teaching job.

'Now I can do all these things, but it's taken me a long time to realize it. It's taking me a long time to get back into being myself.

'If I wanted to sum up my marriage in a few words, I would describe it as 10 years down the salt mines. I'm not saying that every minute was horrible, or that Jenny was a dreadful person – she's not. But she didn't see what I wanted, and I didn't see it either.

'She loved me for being unusual, as she saw it – and then

tried to mould me into a typical husband and father. But I wouldn't go.

'Since becoming single, I've contacted all my former buddies, and have re-established friendships with them. They might come to my place, or I'll go to theirs, and we can talk if we want to, until three in the morning. That would never have been possible with my wife.'

The big problem, Paul says, is that as a husband and father, he had status which he has now lost. 'I was the more important person in the marriage, if I'm to be honest. Everything revolved around me. Now that support system has gone, it's hard to adjust to not being the centre of somebody else's life. But I see now that it's an unhealthy way to live, and it didn't do me any real good.

'The only thing I really miss is having someone to cuddle up to at night. I don't really like sleeping alone, although I like living alone. But I now know there's a very high price to pay for that permanent partner in the bed.'

# Alan

Alan, 47, was married at 21 and divorced 22 years later. He is a journalist on a leading Sunday paper and has two sons aged 24 and 22. For the past 12 years he has followed a highly disciplined spiritual path and because he now wants to develop this further, sees a close relationship as unlikely in the future.

He says: 'Looking back, I realized I used close personal relationships as an anaesthetic, not just in my marriage but in my early family life as well. Even in the domestic setting as a child, I felt that family life was a kind of anaesthetic. We would do things together, watch the TV together and there was nothing wrong in that of course, but there was something wrong with me in that I always wanted to escape from myself.

'Even in those days, I was using those relationships to avoid facing things about myself, things that if I'm to find personal fulfilment and a sense of growth, I've got to face.

'I'm not saying that everybody with a family has these things to face, or blots out important aspects of themselves. It's possible to share and lead a pleasant existence. But for me, even if that were the case, I would find it too narrow an existence and very limiting.'

Alan says he doesn't feel he was subject to external pressures to marry and have a family himself, but that it came naturally and readily to him to enter into a long-term close relationship with just one other person. 'I was aware of wanting it and as our relationship developed, I felt it was the most natural thing in the world. I really enjoyed family life, but looking back, I feel there were a lot of escapist elements, and that my expectations of what the relationship could provide were false and unrealistic.

'It was very much as though I wanted to lose myself in another person, and merge completely. I was keen that our finances should be merged and that decision making should be shared. This sounds all right, but I was always doomed to frustration because such merging simply was not possible. The fact it, you can't merge with another human being and if you try to as a couple, it will be phoney.

'Looking back, I think that we formed a kind of power axis where two articulate people working with words were able to have a supportive attitude towards each other's world views which others could find bullying or threatening. There was a kind of power in numbers. My former wife was a journalist on the same paper.

'I found this all very supportive but the fact is, it doesn't strengthen you as a person. And as time goes on, there is an ever greater fear that the relationship might end.'

For Alan, the most positive aspect of being single is the return of self-respect. 'For the first time in my adult life, I'm standing on my own feet. I've done some of my best work since being single and I have vastly more friends. When I developed a deep interest in yoga and meditation there were terrible sources of conflict, as my wife wasn't interested and I wished she was.

'Once I became single I was freed from this debilitating inner tension. Now, I can have gatherings of 50 or 60 people in my flat and I love it. Beforehand, I had to deal with a grumpy partner, and it was horrible.

'I'm also pleased to discover that self-maintenance is perfectly straightforward and easy. I cook all my own meals and enjoy that very much. I get up and go to bed when I like. For me, the positive aspects have been: saving of energy through not having to deal with conflict of interests; the growth of self-respect, and the loss of the anaesthetic. I realize now that we wasted a lot of time gossiping and chatting and we became very self-indulgent.

'The main difficulty for me was that I lost my family – my wife and two sons – all in one go. My sons went to live with their mother and although they were grown up and at university, I missed family life very much at first.

'I was also surprised at the amount of pain I felt when the

anaesthetic was removed. There were definite withdrawal symptoms which I didn't acknowledge properly. Also, I was going home after a busy day at work to a cold, empty house. Previously there had been warmth and cooking and conversation. For a time, it all seemed very bleak, and I tried to bridge the gap with having people to stay with me. But that didn't work out.

'They were nice enough people, but I was actually missing my wife more than I realized. Now, though, I would never go back into a relationship. I feel so strongly that I have a responsibility to myself and to take that anaesthetic again would be quite unthinkable.'

# Susie

Susie is in her mid-fifties. She had a brief marriage in her youth and has been single for more than 30 years. After a successful career as a writer and broadcaster, she now runs her own PR company and also works as a counsellor. She brought up her son, now a doctor, as a single parent.

She says: 'I didn't really intend to be single all my adult life. When my marriage ended in 1960 I thought it had all been a terrible mistake and that I would soon find somebody more suitable and marry again.

'But although over the years I've had oodles of opportunities to marry, I've never taken them. I always had in the back of my mind that I would marry again some day, but when it came to it, I was always reluctant to give up my freedom. I had actually planned what would be my perfect marriage set-up – separate flats, with a big communal living room, and separate dining rooms, bedrooms and bathrooms.

'I now think that although at the back of my mind I thought I'd remarry, at the front of my mind I didn't really want to. I think I wasn't prepared to compromise, and the package just didn't add up.'

The advantages of being single, says Susie, are that she has very many more friends than she could possibly have as part of a couple, and enjoys relationships with people of all ages, social classes and educational backgrounds. 'When you are in a couple, you insulate yourself, and unwittingly cut yourself off from many experiences and friendships. People often ask me how I know so many people, but of course it's because I'm single.

'There's no doubt that you always lose friends when you become a couple. When you get married, you automatically drop certain friends. Whenever in the past, I've got close to remarrying, I've had to ask myself: do I really want to take on his friends and family?

'But although I have lots of friends, I also like being on my own, and I don't think I could give that up for the sake of having somebody permanent in my life. I now think that freedom is far more important to me than anything else.

'The main drawback is that whether you like it or not, society is organized for couples. I resent having to pay single supplements when I go on holiday, and having to pay more for everything just because I'm not one half of a couple.

'Also, as a South African who came to the UK as a young adult, I don't have friends from childhood and college to contact. I've had to work harder to get to know people than if I were married. Anybody who wants to enter English society from outside almost has to marry to become accepted. It's a fact that people in Britain are far more class-ridden and male-dominated than most of Europe or America.

'It seems to me that marriage gives social status to a woman. In the past, a woman's only entrée into society was to marry, and this has not quite disappeared. You do tend to get marginalized as a single person, especially as you get older. I've seen this happen with many single friends. And as a single woman, you are often subject to harassment from men who can't seem to understand that you prefer to be single.

'In the single world, nobody really has status, as society functions so much as couples. But as an outsider, I can see what most people's relationships are really like, underneath all the pretence and fantasy. Few are any good, really. And increasingly I'm finding that women with a successful career simply don't want men in their lives – they find them too much of a nuisance.

'Often when I'm invited to social functions, I half want to go, but I think of getting there, finding a parking space and then walking into a room full of strangers. If I had somebody to go with, we'd gee each other up. As a single person, you have to be a self-starter all the time.'

Susie says she worked out her holiday plan many years ago. 'I would never go on a package holiday because I might not like anybody in the group. So what I do is to contact friends in different places in the world and ask if I can stay with them. This means I have a base to operate from, and can be alone at the same time as having congenial company. I also go away for four and five day breaks with a friend.

'People often ask me how I'm going to manage in my old age without a partner. But you can never guarantee that you'll both be around. One of you might suddenly die, and you'd still be on your own. I'd never get married or form a permanent relationship just because I was afraid of being lonely in my old age.'

# Karl

Karl, 36, a musician and gay man, says he would like to find the ideal relationship, but reluctantly feels it is probably impossible.

He says: 'Until I was in my late 20s, I spent most of my time trying to have wonderful relationships. I have never been to bed with a woman, but when I was 21 I nearly got engaged, so great were the pressures on me to get married.

'As it was, I was celibate until I was 26, when I had a series of relationships of varying intensity. But always, I felt completely insecure in the relationship and had a great fear that it would end. I did everything I could to make myself feel secure – and I never did.

'Now, I'm sharing a house with another guy, but we don't have any kind of relationship – it's just a convenient arrangement. As a musician travelling the world playing concerts, it's okay for me to be single – I'm kind of excused. People in my home town often ask my mother whether I'm married – the ones who don't realize I'm gay, and she tells them I'm married to my music.'

Karl believes that most people enter into relationships at times when they don't have a clear purpose or aim in life, for just this reason. 'Getting entangled is a way of filling up the time. But my experience of relationships is that I denied myself in order to preserve the relationship. I think that sensitive types of people do.

'One of the main problems is that nobody knows for sure what relationships are supposed to be, or what we want them to achieve. In fact, there's no sense of achievement at all when in a relationship. People believe they are achieving something, but it's all a fantasy.

'If you do achieve the feat of staying together, it's usually at the expense of at least one of you paying a huge price and compromising all the time. You have to weigh up the work involved in maintaining a relationship against your own self-respect.

'It seems to me that while you are committed to another person, it's actually impossible to develop a clear sense of self. I liken it to being addicted to coffee. If you drink five cups a day, you have no idea you are addicted. But try going for two weeks without it – and you soon understand your addiction to the substance.

'My own experience of being single is that it articulated a vacuum in my own personality. I was conscious of the vacuum, and tried to fill it up with love. Yet the force behind that love was emptiness. Only you can learn to love yourself, and the fact is that no relationship is ever guaranteed to last longer than the next minute.

'The reality is that all intimate relationships are based on total insecurity. They mean that you have to deny yourself, and when this happens, it is actually impossible to retain your self-respect. Relationships are a way of wallpapering over the cracks in your personality – for a time it all looks all right, but then the cracks appear again. You haven't really repaired the damage.

'I was a prime candidate for intimate relationships because I was very needy. So what happened is that I found other needy people. It got so bad that I was actually prepared to give up my career for the right relationship. I wanted to prove that I was lovable, and when I had sex with somebody, that meant I was attractive and lovable.

'I now look at heterosexual couples, and see so-called happily married people trading off each other. Often when they're young, the men are dominant and bully and boss the women. Then when they get older, the man is tired and worn out, but the woman is still strong and energetic. So the roles are reversed, with the woman taking all the power. It's always one up, one down.

'But I shall enjoy getting old as a single person. If you think about it, there'll be a lot of us about, and we can all be friends with each other, instead of sealed off in one-to-one units. With friendships, you don't get on each other's nerves and there is no feeling of ownership, of incompleteness.

'I think most relationships happen because people are trying to fulfil an undeveloped part of themselves. The problem is, that's not the way to do it. Relationships provide a crutch, but they don't enable you to walk.

'People are addicted to relationships and to sex, because that way they imagine they can feel love. But nothing lives up to expectations for long, and the only way to keep sex exciting with the same partner is to go for ever more bizarre acts. This is the case with both gay and straight people, whatever so-called sexologists may say to the contrary.'

Although now committed to staying single, Karl believes that relationships are the ideal. 'It would be lovely to have a relationship based on sharing and mutual respect, rather than ownership, jealousy and possessiveness. I know I'm not ready for that – but of course with my music, I have a fulfilling career. I never get lonely because I can always practise, and get closer to a favourite piece of classical music.

'Also, in the musician's world, there is plenty of companionship. If I wasn't involved in a way of life that actively supported my personal growth, then I definitely would be in a relationship. In times of weakness, I sometimes wish I had somebody there to share things with, somebody to take responsibility away from me.

'It's a complete myth, though, that other people can take care of you.' Karl feels that people who think like him are in a great minority. 'I've learned that the only way I can regain self-respect is to find it within myself. I'm never going to find it through a relationship.

'Of course, it's more difficult for gay people, because we are outside society's norms anyway. For this reason, perhaps, there's a greater urge to band together. Some people tell me that it's unnatural and against religion to be gay, but I tell them it's natural for me. I probably could have a sexual relationship with a woman if I really had to – I think most gay men could – but it would always feel wrong, always unnatural.

'And it would be so unfair on the woman, although very many gay men do get married and have families.

'I think the only way to work towards genuine integration and harmony within oneself is to be single. It's the only way you can find out who you are, what your real needs are, and to develop your own personal potential.

'Very single-minded and strong people may be able to do

this within a relationship. If so, then they wouldn't be putting much work into the relationship – that would be the job of the other person. Great male musicians, male artists, can do fine work when in a relationship – but the other person will always suffer, always have to come second and deny themselves.

'Unfortunately, there was a tendency for this in myself, and it's one reason why I could never combine a relationship with my work – the work would automatically take second place. Then I could easily feel I had lost everything and gained very little.'

# Gill

Gill, 39, was single for 12 years after her first marriage ended. She has two teenage children from her first marriage and just a year ago married Charlie, a man she had known for nearly 20 years. Charlie, also divorced, has four children from his first marriage.

Gill says: 'I never thought I would ever get married again. Although I did not seek or want a divorce, I got used to living on my own. I trained for a career in social work and had lots of friends and colleagues, after the initial shock died down.

'I bought a little cottage in the country, and gradually did it up until it was perfect. Then Charlie, a doctor whom I had known as a teenager, came into my life, and we decided to go on holiday together, just as friends.

'We got on so well during that holiday that when we came back, we decided to get married.'

So how has it worked out? Gill says: 'I wondered what I would have to give up, and what I would be gaining. I think I felt that I'd never had a proper relationship, because my first husband was very dominant. He was more educated than me, older and earned far more money than I ever could.

'During the years I was single, I went on many personal growth courses, and learned relaxation and meditation. I also attended, for a time, a woman's consciousness-raising group, and these all opened my eyes to aspects of myself that had been shut off before.

'It seemed the most natural thing in the world for us to get married, but if I'm to be honest, my life has become far more complicated and I'm finding myself having to make compromises. For instance, Charlie's children often come to stay, and when my own are with us as well, that means I've got eight people to cook for, which I could well do without.

'I don't think I realized fully what I was taking on when I married Charlie. But I felt the need for closeness, companionship, and also somebody to love. I do feel I've sold out among the sisterhood for getting married again, and partly for that reason, I've moved away from my previous home to a new area.

'We have definitely decided not to have any more children, and that's a relief. But although we get on so well, there has been a price to pay. I've had to cope with Charlie's ex-wife and her problems, not to mention the maintenance he pays, and which has made it necessary for me to get a better-paying job, and I've also now lost many of the single women friends I had before. Those cosy evenings are now out.

'It all seemed a good idea at the time, but now I think I was probably on my own for too long to be able to settle back easily into a husband-and-wife type relationship. It's been a more difficult year than I imagined, and my own children aren't too happy at the new arrangement, even though they quite like Charlie. They're not keen on his children being there, though, and this has caused friction.

'Because I have grown up so much in the years I had to cope alone, I have quite a different relationship with Charlie from the one I had with my first husband, who dominated me all the time. Our relationship is more equal and far more sharing. Also, we have a strong rapport, which was never the case in my first marriage.

'But even so, there are compromises to be made, and I'm never on my own now. There's a completely different feel about "our" house than the one I lived in on my own – it's got "our" things in rather than just my things. I've also learned how isolating it can be to be married again.

'When I was single, I had lots of single friends. Now, I'm mixing again with other married couples. It all takes a lot of getting used to, but I felt I needed to experience living with somebody in a different, more equal and sharing way after the years of singleness.'

# 4

# Myths About Being Single
# – And The Reality

I f you are newly single, about to become single, considering being single – or wondering whether this is a
lifetime's state for you, now's the time to divest yourself of
some favourite but damaging myths about the single life –
and replace them with the positive reality.

**MYTH:** You get lonely on your own.

**REALITY:** You are just as likely to be lonely with a partner
you can no longer talk to, and with whom you no longer
share any real views. The idea that marriage or other long-
term relationship is a cure for loneliness is a widely-held
myth. The reality is that if you are lonely, or feel lonely,
you will attract another lonely, needy person to you – and
the whole problem will be compounded.

Fear of loneliness is probably the most powerful reason
which propels people into relationships, and keeps them
there long after the relationship has ceased to have any
real meaning. The message should be, rather: never, ever

even consider going into a relationship if you feel lonely. Make an effort instead to develop and cultivate more detached friendships. So often, lonely people just hope that somehow, somewhere, there will be the right person who will lift them out of their loneliness for ever. Not true. Only you can cure your loneliness – and that will happen when you stop being afraid of it, and no longer believe it is something which must inevitably be corrected by having one special other person in our lives.

**MYTH:** Your social life will dry up when you're single.

**REALITY:** All the single people I know have a far *more* exciting social life than those who are married or in intimate relationships. The presence of a permanent partner in your life tends to make you lazy, and to look at each other, criticizing and complaining, rather than being outward-looking and extrovert. A whole world of freedom becomes available to you when you're single, when there's no spouse to pour cold water on your ideas, who doesn't want you to play golf, go to football matches, drink in the pub or go to evening classes to improve your skills. There will be nobody to cook a meal for, nobody to have to explain things to – and the best thing is that you can invite people to your house without wondering whether your spouse will approve, or complain because you have messed up their proposed quiet evening in front of the TV.

Being single gives you a chance to develop your hobbies and interests, whatever these may be – joining a bridge club, learning a new language, going to car maintenance classes, or spreading your needlework or dressmaking all over the living room floor. There will be nobody to tell you to clear up, nobody to criticize what you want to do – and you can have the social life that you've always wanted. Don't be nervous that there won't be any like-minded people in the world out there – there will, plenty.

But, if you are newly single, it will all take some time to build up. Don't expect your telephone initially to be forever ringing with fabulous invitations. It will take time for you to get out of the habit of being one of a couple, and to establish yourself as an independent, autonomous person. Also, it may feel strange at first for you to be doing things on your own, to have all that freedom to please yourself. But before you know where you are, you will be used to it.

As a single person, you do certainly have to try harder to have a good social life – but the rewards are very great.

**MYTH:** Nobody cares about you when you're single.

**REALITY:** It's possible to have *more* friends who care about you when you're single than with just one person, who may get have got so used to you over the years that you have become almost like a piece of furniture, a permanent fixture. It's all too easy for spouses actually to stop caring about each other, so don't imagine that just because you don't have that one special person, you are lacking somebody who will automatically care for you. You will find that your genuine friends do want to help you out, and are concerned for your welfare, not just because they might want a similar service if they need support – but because they will want to stand by you.

I've certainly found that friends rally round eagerly when you need them – and I'm happy to support them when I can. That is the good thing about friendship; friends can be there when needed, but they do not have to be there all the time. Because the relationship is that much more detached, it has every chance of being much healthier.

In order to be a friend, get into the habit of telephoning your single friends and having a chat with them. There doesn't always have to be a reason for ringing, and you can always preface any conversation with a question as to whether this is a convenient time to call.

Most people find when they become single that their circle of caring friends expands enormously. But don't expect everyone to care – you will find that friendships are of differing strengths, and also some personalities are more 'caring' than others.

**MYTH:** Single women aren't welcome at dinner parties.

**REALITY:** Any lively, interesting person of any age or either sex is extremely welcome at gatherings such as dinner parties. The reason single women are not apparently welcome is if they have previously been invited only because of their husband's position or status – they automatically lose that connection on becoming single. This has led to the idea that an older woman – one who is ditched for a younger model – is cast out of society, without a proper place.

If you, as a newly single woman, have always lived vicariously, then for a time it might be the case that invitations stop coming. Ask yourself whether this is because you were simply the 'Mrs' on your husband's invitations, and that if you hadn't been married to him, you would never have been asked in your own right.

But the same goes for men who have been invited only because of who their wives are – although this is, or has been up till now, far rarer than the other way round.

It may be that, as a single person, you get invited to far fewer dinner parties than when you were married. This is because dinner parties are *par excellence* 'couple' affairs – but before bemoaning this, ask yourself how many of those dinner parties you actually enjoyed, and how many you went to, or even gave, because you were expected to, and to return favours.

The way to continue the dinner party habit, if you want to, is to start holding them on your own. Ask just the people you want to be with, and don't be afraid of all-female or all-male parties. Forget about gender, and don't worry if there are too many males or too many females to have complete equality.

When I first became single, I instituted all-female dinner parties, and they were a great success. Some of my still-married female friends initially felt rather odd about women-only affairs, wondering whether they should dress up and wear make-up, if 'only' women were going to be there. But without exception, they have found them extremely enjoyable, because it's an opportunity to talk without interruption, about the things that interest women. We have noticed that the vibes change dramatically when there is a man present.

You will probably find, as time goes on, that you start a completely new network of friends, many of whom do not fall into the conventional couple mode. But these days, there are so many divorced and separated people, and also many couples who live together for convenience only, but who have separate social lives, that you will discover your dinner parties are that much more interesting and lively than the deadening couple-only affairs, where so often partners bicker, the men talk to each other and the women talk to each other, and marital arguments and disputes develop. So often, when long-married couples are invited together, they have completely forgotten the other exists as a separate person, and interrupt them, talk over their heads, ignore them altogether.

'Cosy-couple' dinner parties are often not such wonderful affairs as they might seem – and certainly don't be afraid that your social life is going to dry up because nobody will want your company any more. As you establish new friendships, you will find that you meet many new and interesting people, people who you would probably never have got to know when you were a couple.

And don't forget – you can always invite just one person round for supper, a drink, or tea – it doesn't always have to be a full-scale *haute cuisine* dinner party! Food can be simple, and easily prepared.

**MYTH:** I'll never get over the feeling of being left, of being dumped.

**REALITY:** Yes you will. Although it is always a shock when one partner announces that they've had enough and want to leave, if you've been vigilant you will have seen the signs coming for some time. Even terrible grief, it is estimated, such as when a loved one dies, lasts at its height for about two years. Then life begins again, and you start to feel normal.

The point is that if one person wants to leave the partnership, it is effectively over anyway, and there is no point in trying to pretend it can still be patched up. It will always come down to one person, though, to be the one who leaves, to be the one who says they want out. What you really have to cope with is feelings of rejection and hurt ego: why should he/she want to leave wonderful *me*? Many people can't understand it at all.

Of course unexpected widowhood is always hard to bear – but even here, the grief doesn't last for ever. Don't ever imagine, though, that the cure for the emptiness left in your life when an intimate partner leaves it, for whatever reason, is to fill it up with somebody else. It is far more rewarding to discover who you are, to become complete in yourself without needing anybody else to 'complete' you.

People can often feel they are only halves, not fully-integrated, whole human beings when they are suddenly left – but this is an indication of how much they had come to rely on that other person.

In our present society, we confuse love and attachment, assuming them to be the same thing. But attachment happens when you bind yourself to another person out of fear or feelings of inadequacy, whereas love is when you can let people go, let them be free.

Anybody who has been suddenly left needs time to come to terms with the sense of grief, loss and betrayal – you can also feel betrayed when somebody close to you has died. Feelings of all kinds need to be acknowledged, and dealt with as they arise. It is only by admitting feelings, going with the emotions, and working through them, talking about how you feel, that the negative feelings concerning your loss can be turned, ultimately, into positive ones. People who have never 'got over' the loss of somebody dear to them are those who have never allowed themselves to work through their feelings – which may be far more complicated than ever imagined.

**MYTH:** I'll never have sex again.

**REALITY:** Now that AIDS is upon us, 'sex experts' have been writing endlessly about the virtues of marriage and monogamy, extolling the benefits of a close, loving, sex life within the confines of a committed relationship. This can make those who are single feel left out – but the truth is that there is nothing easier than to have sex if you really want it. Like lonely people, two people avid for sex will easily find each other.

The idea of 'casual sex', once so popular, is now going out of fashion, officially, although there is no real evidence that people are doing it any less than they were in the sixties.

True, when you are single, there is not a convenient sex partner always handy – but was there anyway, really? If you have come out of a relationship, be honest and you'll probably admit to yourself that sex wasn't all that wonderful for much of the time, and caused at least as many problems as it solved.

The wonder of being single is that there is no constant pressure to perform, nobody to say no to, no need to hope against hope that tonight won't be the night – and nobody to get tired of as the years go by. The fact is, most single people have a far better sex life than married people or those in a committed partnership, simply because it happens less often, therefore it's more special, and both of you will make more effort. It seems to me that the biggest myth about our current society is that sex with the same person can get better and better as the years go by. I don't know of any relationship where this has happened.

The truth is that sex is, or can be, very exciting with a new partner, but as you get used to that partner, the sex becomes ever more mundane and ordinary.

When people become single after extricating themselves from long-term partnerships, they often discover that sex is not such a fundamental need as it seemed. And if you don't like sex, or don't want it, you have the freedom not to do it – which may be difficult when you are in a long-term relationship.

**MYTH:** I'll miss having somebody to cuddle up to at night.

**REALITY:** This is unlikely, once you get used to being on your own. I would say that sleeping alone is probably the greatest fear that keeps people tied into relationships. The fact is that sleeping with somebody can, like anything else, become such a habit that sleeping on your own feels extremely strange. Certainly, it can be nice, it can be extremely comforting, to have a warm body next to you in bed, but ask yourself what price you have to pay for the constant presence of somebody else. It is not true that when you are single you will lose all close physical contact, something we all enjoy from time to time.

But if sleeping with somebody appears to be a need, rather than something which is enjoyable once in a while, ask yourself why you should feel this need, why you feel so afraid to be on your own.

After many years of sleeping with a partner, newly-single people can feel very strange when on their own. But most people discover, once they've got used to it, that they prefer it – it's cleaner, you sleep better, it's more peaceful, and there is more freedom to go to bed and get up just when you choose.

And don't forget that being single does not mean that you will never have anybody in bed with you again. It simply means that you will be able to choose when and whom, rather than having to sleep in the same bed as somebody just because you are in that kind of relationship.

**MYTH:** I can't cope on my own.

**REALITY:** Yes you can! The fact is that being in a long-term relationship tends to take away our abilities to cope with many everyday tasks, so that we can imagine they are way beyond us. Every extra thing you cope with imparts self-confidence and self-esteem. Any reasonably intelligent person can learn to cook a meal, park a car, pay bills on time, dust and vacuum. There's simply nothing to it.

**MYTH:** I'm afraid I won't be able to manage money on my own.

**REALITY:** Anybody can manage money on their own. Like coping with household tasks, there's simply nothing to it. What often happens in a relationship is that one person takes responsibility for the finances and, because of this, they can come to seem a financial wizard. It is unlikely that they are, and much more likely that they don't know any more about money than anybody else.

The truth is, hardly any of us are financial geniuses. Some people have the ability to elevate financial matters into some kind of mystique whereby they try to maintain there's some arcane knowledge involved, accessible only to the few. But look at how often in recent years empires and big businesses have crumbled owing millions of pounds. These concerns have been able to employ the best, or most expensive, financial brains – and they've still gone down the drain.

Nobody has a crystal ball, nobody can look into the future and advise you on a good financial decision. For instance, in the UK for the past twenty-five or thirty years, property has been a wonderful investment and, because of inflation, money in the bank has not kept up its value.

Now all this has changed, and many of us are stuck with houses we can't afford and can't sell. *Nobody foresaw any of this*. It is of course true that some people make lots of money, others spend it wildly, some people are frugal and thrifty, others incredibly generous. It is a distinct possibility that if you have left financial matters to your partner, you don't actually know what kind of attitude you have towards money. Only by becoming single do you discover your individuality so far as money is concerned.

For instance, when I was married, I just assumed that my husband and myself had an identical attitude towards money. Both of us had completely trusted the other in financial matters, and together we took calculated risks on houses and jobs.

It wasn't until we separated that I came to understand that we actually had very different approaches. While my ex-husband is careful and tends to be frugal and hoarding, my personality is that of a risk-taker, a hustler, somebody who seems to have to live on some kind of financial edge. The careful allotting of bits of money to this and that, living well within one's income rather than trying to increase income, is not for me.

Also, when married, I just assumed, as many women do, that I was no good with money, that I just let it slip through my fingers. Now I have to make ends meet, or try to, I've discovered that I'm just as good with money as anybody else, and have as astute a grasp on financial matters as those who purport to advise me, who as often as not know nothing. I'm thinking here of banks, accountants, financial advisers of all kinds. Mainly, they just want to take ever bigger bits of money off you.

Being single gives you a chance to come to terms with your own attitudes towards money and to learn, with pleasure, that you can cope with it perfectly well.

**MYTH:** I'll never be able to earn a living on my own.

**REALITY:** You will if you grow up. The terror of having to earn their own living, being completely responsible for themselves and not having anybody to give them hand-outs is what keeps many women locked into relationships they would otherwise like to leave. The terror is increased if you've never earned your own living before, or if you know that what you bring in would not possibly keep the household in the way it's been accustomed to run.

Very often, though, these terrors are more apparent than real. Several years ago, American author Colette Dowling drew attention to women's hidden fear of independence in her book *The Cinderella Complex* where, she said, even high-earning, high-achieving women were still somewhere yearning for a handsome prince who would come and take them away from all this. One very successful businesswoman friend of mine, whose company turns over £5 or £6 million a year, said that she is *still* unconsciously waiting for a man to come and shoulder responsibility, take all her worries away. She knows it won't happen – but the feeling remains, deep inside her.

In the past, there were very practical reasons for women not daring to be on their own. Even nowadays, it is a fact that single, divorced and separated women are less well off than men in a similar position. But the fact is, things are changing all the time. If you have never worked for money and have dependent children, you will be entitled to a good share of the joint proceeds in a divorce, plus maintenance for the children. Of course, many men are notorious for not paying maintenance, so the thing is here to make sure you are satisfied with what you get at the time of divorce or separation. The 'clean break' is increasingly becoming the norm when people split up.

Nowadays, it is often the men who are nervous about not being able to manage. They see their standard of living plummet when the relationship breaks up, as they will probably have to share everything with their former partner and it is a fact that two people apart cannot live so cheaply as two together, on the same money.

Nowadays, though, there is more opportunity than ever before for women to become self-sufficient financially. There are courses you can take (on managing money or avoiding debt, for example), if you have a spare room you can let it out to a lodger (not a happy solution for everybody, but possibly something to consider for the short term), you can upgrade your skills or go back to the profession you once had.

Once you have courage to end a relationship, you will most probably discover that the financial situation isn't as bad as you may have feared – but you may well have to face the fact that there will be less money available. Now you alone, not both of you, will have to find money for the mortgage, the gas and electricity bills, the car, the telephone. It can be hard at first, particularly if you're not used to it, but as with all other aspects of becoming single, you will soon become amazed and delighted at your ability to cope.

**MYTH:** I need somebody.

**REALITY:** Nobody 'needs' anybody at all. The fact is that we are all whole people on our own and we do not need others to complete us, or to provide what we ourselves consider we lack. No other person can make up a lack in yourself; no other person can give you power, security, a sense of belonging.

**MYTH:** Living on my own will be boring.

**REALITY:** It will be far more exciting. Most single people I know have much more interesting and varied lives than those who remain in exclusive relationships. Being single seems to open out the world, and it tends to close when we form intimate, exclusive relationships. Even in small towns or villages, there is probably a wealth of things to do, people to meet, that you haven't even begun to tap.

**MYTH:** There's more security when you share your life with somebody.

**REALITY:** Nonsense! The myth of security is probably the biggest myth of all time. However tied up you may be with your partner, the fact of the matter is that he or she may be run over by a bus tomorrow, leave you for somebody else, get ill, get lost at sea. There is never any guarantee whatsoever that this person you are tied up will be with you for even 24 hours, let alone a lifetime. And the more you associate feelings of security with an intimate relationship, the more devastated you will be when it finally ends – as all relationships will, eventually.

**MYTH:** You're nobody until somebody loves you.

**REALITY:** You're less likely to be somebody when some-body loves you, as the chances are you will become dependent and clinging, and your coping mechanisms will disappear. The reality is that you are somebody whether anybody loves you or not.

**MYTH:** If you're single, this must mean you are unattractive.

**REALITY:** Have you looked around lately? If so, you'll see that all sorts of extremely unattractive people are in couples – the grey-haired, elderly, balding, fat, ugly – and not just unattractive in looks, either. All kinds of monstrously unattractive people get married and form relationships. There is always somebody equally unattractive for the unattractive to attach themselves to – people tend to go to their own level, except when there is a powerful trade-off involved, such as when beautiful young models 'fall in love' with elderly millionaires.

Also, if you look around, you will notice that it's the *single* people who are most probably well-groomed, attractive, smartly dressed. Very many long-married people I know who have come out of relationships say that one of the first things they did on becoming single was to improve their appearance – get new clothes, new hairstyles, join a health club and so on. It's those in long-term relationships who tend to let themselves go, feeling as the years go by that it's not worth making an effort for somebody who has become such a permanent fixture.

The fact is, single people are intriguing, interesting – and far more so than those locked into one-to-one relationships.

**MYTH:** Life will be horrible with nobody to share the ups and downs with.

**REALITY:** Don't make the mistake of imagining that not having somebody glued permanently to your side will mean that you won't have anybody to share your triumphs and tragedies with. It's just that it may not always be the same person. And how many long-term marriages do you know where partners no longer have anything in common with each other at all – and share nothing? Very often, intimate partners are not that interested in what you do, as they have long ceased to regard you as a separate individual.

**MYTH:** I'm worried about what my mother/friends/ neighbours might think if I'm single all my life.

**REALITY:** They are probably, as singer Cliff Richard said, secretly envious – but daren't show it in case it makes them look too closely at their own life. Also, you can't know for sure what anybody else is thinking, and you may be simply foisting your own fears and ideas onto them.

I hope this list of myths and realities will go some way to clearing up the confusion that people often have when they contemplate the single life. True, it does often seem an odd choice in a world full of couples, and in a society where we are fully expected to couple up with somebody at some stage.

But I feel a definite consciousness shift is happening, where at last we are beginning to see how tyrannical the couple mentality can be, how stifling for the individual, and how fearful it can make individuals considering striking out on their own. The fact is that few, if any, who have become single after years of living in a relationship ever regret it.

There will of course be ups and downs – nobody can be up all the time. But the important thing is that your feelings and emotions will no longer be anaesthetized all the time – and you will be able to reclaim yourself for yourself, rather than giving away bits of yourself to other people.

And as all the myths fall away, and you come to see for yourself what paper tigers your fears are – you may well wonder why you didn't have the courage to become single years ago. For singleness is not just a matter of not having an intimate partner; it's also a matter of how you view yourself – as a kind of Sleeping Beauty waiting to be woken by a prince (or princess), or as somebody complete and independent.

# 5
# Learning To Be Single

The most overwhelming emotion confronting newly-single people is fear. Even if you have decided in theory that you want to be alone, disentangling yourself from a long-term partnership can still be hard.

How do you set about discovering yourself, and keep your head above water financially and emotionally? How do you learn to swim without your life raft, walk without crutches?

The fears seem no less great whether you have been suddenly left, whether you have made up your mind to leave a long-term partnership or even if you are wondering whether you will *ever* become part of a couple, or be single for the rest of your life. Very many single people are actually putting their lives on hold, believing that they will have a wonderful relationship at some stage in their lives – or not quite liking to let the idea go.

Nobody can ever know what will happen in the future, of course, but it's as well to learn the skills required to exist as a single person, even if for no other reason than we have no idea when it might happen to us. The fact is, singleness can strike at any minute, however firmly locked and bonded relationships seem to be.

Professional counsellors believe that the two most difficult areas of life to cope with are dramatic change and loss, events which so often go together. Becoming single after many years of togetherness involves both of these, and can be considered a major life change or rite of passage. For very many people, becoming single will involve selling and moving house, a major upheaval in itself. It may also involve moving to another area and will, in any case, require learning a whole new set of skills.

There will also probably be financial worries. One of the reasons why newly-single people experience financial difficulties, even when both separated partners are earning good salaries, is that when everything is joint, each partner tends to forget about the other, and imagine it is all theirs. The reality: 'We own a house worth half a million' can easily come to mean: '*I* own a house worth half a million' – a very different thing. Many people on the point of becoming single would love nothing more than for the partner to vanish into thin air, leaving them with all the assets – house, insurance, furniture, record collection, and so on.

Unfortunately, this rarely happens, except in the very unusual circumstances of one partner simply walking out and disappearing. The more material assets there are, the less likely this is to happen. The other partner usually wants half, at least, of the joint assets, believing this to be fair. The difficulty is for both parties to agree on what is fair, especially if only one wants out, as often happens.

The vagaries of the present legal system mean that, unless everything was clearly set out in writing beforehand, dividing the joint assets depends on what each party – or their lawyers – consider fair under the circumstances. And very often it's arbitrary indeed.

The bottom line for many people considering splitting up is to ask yourself: if I were to get nothing at all, would I still want to become single, be free? If the answer comes out resoundingly 'yes' – then you will find the courage to proceed.

Margaret, for instance, in the case history in chapter 3, had joint ownership with her husband of a very large house with several acres of valuable land. He did not want a separation or a divorce and definitely did not want to move from the house, which was his pride and joy. As Margaret had no paying career at the time, she had to consider whether she would still want to leave if she got nothing, which was a possibility.

'But there was no choice,' she said. 'I felt that I could support myself and that even if I walked out with nothing, I still had to do it.' In the event, Margaret's lawyers decided that she deserved more than half of the domestic proceeds, as she had spent several years helping her husband build up his business, and had worked as unpaid accountant, PR manager, office manager and hostess until the business was on its feet. Her husband, Bill, did not want to divide up the business, so had no choice but to hand over the lion's share of the money from the house sale over to Margaret.

'This gave me some financial security,' she said. 'But I would still have done it, even if Bill had managed to stay in the house and keep everything.'

Paul's case (also from chapter 3) was rather different. His ex-wife Jenny's lawyers decided that, because as a head of department, he had a better-paid teaching job than she, and because he was more of a 'career' teacher, his earning potential was greater than hers. Also, she had custody of their son Antony, something Paul would not have wanted in any case. The outcome was that Paul was awarded one-fifth of the joint proceeds, and Jenny bought him out, making the joint house entirely hers. But not long after the divorce, which was of the 'clean break' variety, Paul was made redundant. He found it extremely difficult to get a job at the same level, and for a time had to go on income support.

'So much for earning potential,' he said. 'Jenny is now earning considerably more than me, as she soon got a much better job when a teacher in her school left. And I've still only got a fifth.'

None of us knows what might happen – which is why arbitrary assessments of what is 'fair' may have little meaning. People who have built up joint assets over many years of a long relationship have to expect that they may not get all they want, or imagine they deserve financially, when they split up.

I will talk further about financial matters later, as these often loom largest for people contemplating living singly. But the first, and most important consideration, is to start thinking of yourself *mentally* as a single person. Even if you are currently in a relationship, imagine that it could end at any minute, which in fact it could.

Think of yourself as an autonomous, independent individual, rather than as one half, either lesser or greater, of a two-person partnership. It's a lot healthier emotionally than trying to entwine and wrap yourself around somebody else.

# Becoming Single Mentally

The advice given here is the exact opposite to much of that in the dozens of 'have a happy relationship' books, which encourage people to give 'commitment' to their relationships, and to put 'work' into them – whatever that might mean.

The most important person you can give 'commitment' to and put 'work' into is yourself. And that means taking full responsibility for everything you say and do, learning to have and to express opinions, and to start feeling complete in yourself, rather than as if you are missing some vital organ.

The trouble is, most of us are brought up to be dependent and fearful, which is why so many of us marry or form relationships at the earliest opportunity, long before we have properly grown up, or given ourselves a chance to exist independently. The main reason we are so ready to form tightly-sealed units is because we are afraid to take responsibility for ourselves, afraid of expressing a direct opinion.

The best way to begin separating yourself, to start thinking of yourself as an independently-operating individual, is to start learning to say 'I' rather than 'we' – a surprisingly difficult thing for very many people. If you have never got into the habit of saying 'I', practising this may feel very strange at first, almost like being in a foreign country where you do not know the language.

If you don't believe how difficult most people find it to say 'I', just sit and listen to an average married couple talking. See how often they say 'we' and how rarely they say 'I', even when expressing what is supposed to be an individual opinion.

In counselling parlance, saying 'I' is to own what you say, being strong-minded enough to stand up and be counted for your actions and thoughts. If you say 'we' all the time, this means you are not taking responsibility, and are trying to give the impression that you are part of an indissoluble unit, an undivided front – which may not be the case in reality. If you say 'one' like the Queen and the Royal Family, this means you are trying to universalize your individual experience. It's just as bad as saying 'we' all the time, although it may sound posher.

And if you say 'you' as in: 'It makes you very cross, doesn't it, when people let you down', you are pushing your own thoughts and opinions onto the other person, your hearer. If you listen to celebrities and politicians on television, notice how rarely they take responsibility for what they are saying, how very infrequently anybody has the courage actually to own what they say.

How much healthier to say 'I' all the time, when you are referring to what you and you alone are thinking. Make a point of owning your thoughts now, and not pushing them on to your partner, who may not actually hold those views.

Paul, in our case history, said that one thing which made him furious with his former wife was the way she would say to other people (for instance): 'We really enjoyed that film, didn't we, Paul?' He said: 'I always felt tempted to say: well, you might have done, but I certainly didn't. It was as if she was trying to make us some kind of indissoluble unit, and this meant she was forcing opinions and ideas on me which I didn't necessarily hold.'

The next step on the way to becoming mentally single is to have the courage to make your own decisions, even if these turn out not to be for the best, with hindsight. People who are in positions where they have to make very many decisions a day, sometimes several times an hour, such as newspaper editors or politicians, have to take the risk that sometimes, maybe often, they will make the wrong decision – even if they are reluctant to admit it. But they have to make the decisions, and also carry the can for them if they turn out to be wrong.

The same goes, or should go, for all of us. We will all make decisions we regret, hasty decisions, decisions where we feel we have been conned, ripped off, not been careful enough, have not taken the trouble to amass all the facts before going ahead. All human beings do this, however clever they may seem.

*None of this matters.* Few decisions are completely irrevocable and even if they are, you made them in the light of your knowledge, experience and understanding at the time. There is no way of knowing what will happen in the future. But the more decisions you get used to making, the better you will get at making them, and the better your decisions will be, too. Like anything else, learning to make decisions is a skill which can be improved with practice.

If making decisions by yourself is a new idea for you, remember that you don't have to make life-changing ones all at once. You can begin with very small things, like deciding on new saucepans, or new kitchen curtains.

Once you have made one decision, such as a major purchase, all by yourself, you will be empowering yourself to make others. Very many women, for instance, are terrified of buying a car on their own, thinking, erroneously, that men all come with automobile know-how.

They don't. Even the cleverest, most car-crazy men make highly expensive mistakes when buying cars, so don't be fooled. George, for instance, decided to buy a Porsche when, after eight years, his graphic art business started to take off. He was so delighted with being a Porsche owner that after a year, he bought himself a bigger and more powerful one. Then his business went into severe recession and he had to lay workers off. He could no longer afford to run the Porsche and in any case, it didn't look good to be driving such an expensive car when he was making staff redundant.

He decided to sell the vehicle. The only problem was, nobody wanted to buy it and a year later, it was still sitting in the garage unsold – all £28,000 worth of it, money he could well do with to help his business out.

Even if you do buy a car which proves to be a bad buy, so what? You will have learned valuable lessons for the future, and the money you lost may have been necessary to teach you that hard lesson.

Some people find it difficult to go into a shop and buy clothes for themselves, decide on one garment over another. My ex-husband was one of these, along with many men who seem to have to have their wives or girlfriends with them when buying clothes.

When we first separated, he was extremely nervous of going into a shop and choosing garments for himself. Then he hit on the solution, one which has served him well ever since. He discovered what were 'his' colours and styles, and this gave him the confidence to choose for himself. Most people who come into contact with him now consider him to be very well-dressed, even though he buys clothes only when he absolutely has to.

Unless you can learn to buy things for yourself, you will never learn to get your eye in, never know how much of the decision has been yours, and what was the input of somebody else. And what does it matter if you make a few wrong purchases? We are not going to be awarded marks in a big black book somewhere for choosing the wrong colour, the wrong wallpaper or carpet. And bear in mind that having somebody with you doesn't always guarantee a foolproof purchase, either.

But of course, having the courage to make your own decisions extends far further than making domestic or personal purchases. There is nothing wrong with taking advice, so long as you make sure you take it from the experts, people who really know what they are doing, who can be impartial and who are not trying to rip you off at the same time.

When I decided to separate from my husband, I had no idea where to live, no idea what kind of property to look for, no idea what market prices were like in different areas. So I would not really know whether I was looking at a bargain or something highly overpriced.

I didn't want to spend weeks or months looking at unsuitable flats, so I made the decision to go to a professional housefinding firm, people who question you carefully about your circumstances and finances, and then try to find the exact right home for you, taking a commission. I spent a couple of hours with these people, and together we drew up a blueprint of what I wanted.

However, a couple of days later, I was looking in a newspaper, when suddenly 'my' flat stared at me from an advertisement. It was the right price, the right location, had the right number of rooms. I went to look at it instantly and made an offer, which was accepted that day. The flat was in extremely bad decorative condition, and needed some major work on it, but even that was a bonus, as it gave me scope to put my personal stamp on a home for the very first time in my life.

Of course, the flat has not been problem-free – and I had to deal with some severe difficulties such as damp, one of the basement floors flooding, and wondering how on earth to pay the mortgage when interest rates went sky high. But for most of us, the decision to buy a house is one of the biggest ones we will ever make – and even for that, you don't need a permanent partner in your life.

# Special Difficulties for Women

For women, three overwhelming difficulties stand in the way of mental singleness: fear, dependency and timidity – the most confidence-sapping and esteem-lowering emotions anybody can have. Of course men suffer from these emotions too, but usually far less severely than women.

It has been said that the major difficulty facing women who want to live singly is financial. It is certainly true that women are earning on average only 70 per cent of the adult male wage and it is also the case that very many full-time, non-earning wives and mothers wonder how on earth they will manage if they leave their breadwinner husbands. The newspapers abound with stories of women married to violent men who cannot leave because they have no money at all, nowhere to go – and the man keeps promising to reform.

Perhaps the house is in his name, perhaps he is the sole owner or tenant anyway.

All this puts women in an extremely difficult position. But one reason why women are so poverty-stricken, especially when attached to men, is because of our fears about being independent, our desire to become attached. If you haven't earned money for many years it may be a bit late for me to say 'never become financially dependent on anybody' – but it's good always to try and think of yourself as independent of others in the monetary sense.

In the powerful novel by Timothy Mo, *Soursweet*, about a Chinese family coping in London, the non-earning wife makes sure she always puts by a certain amount of 'secret' money from the money her husband brings home from his job in a Chinese restaurant. Every woman who is not earning her own money should try to do this – keep some money for yourself, secretly if you have to, so that you will always at least be able to make a quick getaway.

Many women, even nowadays, mistakenly think they have a 'choice' as to whether to be a full-time stay-at-home wife and mother, or go out to work. Governments, it is said, want women to be earners to collect the extra revenue, so that's why they are trying to persuade women to stay on at work.

But the fact is that nowadays it is far too risky to stop being an earner. Any woman who wants to spend some time with her family should try to make sure she saves up some money *before* reproducing – so that she has always got money of her own. If nothing else, it ensures self-respect. An important aspect of anybody's autonomy is to regard themselves as responsible for themselves financially, whatever may happen. It's an attitude of mind as much as to do with the amount of money you may have in the bank.

But not taking care of oneself financially, depending on somebody else, is all part of the poisonous emotion known as attachment. Attachment, so often wrongly considered praiseworthy, eats into the soul. It starts, probably in very early years, with feelings of low self-esteem and low self-worth. It is, as I have said, basically low self-esteem which makes women attach themselves like limpets to men in the first place, wrongly believing that the men are better earners, stronger, more powerful, more important than any woman could be.

It is attachment that makes us willing and ready to take on a man's name, wiping out our identity. It is attachment that allows us to wear wedding rings, symbols of ownership, to call ourselves 'Mrs' and all the other manifestations of locking ourselves into the identity of another.

Mostly, when we form partnerships with men, we are quite happy to lose an aspect of our identity, so little do we value it. We call ourselves 'Mrs John Smith' so that we don't have to take so much responsibility for ourselves, and so that we can, we hope, gain a new and better identity by subsuming into somebody else. The American feminist writer Gloria Steinem recently drew attention to the terrible problems of low self-esteem which continue to beset women, problems which can start as early as five or six years old, and get worse as the years go by.

It's a problem far more insidious in its way than the patriarchy and social construct which says that it's perfectly all right for a woman to lose her identity completely by merging with a man.

It often seems that the best way for a woman to gain status

is to attach herself to the best male she can find. Women with very low self-esteem, who have little sense of their own worth, may attach themselves to alcoholics, bullies, or violent men, believing they don't deserve anything better, while women with slightly more self-esteem, slightly more self-confidence, may go for the 'alpha' male – somebody tall, good-looking, aristocratic, maybe, and with plenty of money in the bank.

But any attachment by which you hope to gain some kind of status by association is a potent indication of low self-confidence. The paradox is that once you have become prey to attachment, your self-esteem and feelings of self-worth take an even greater dive than when you were unattached. I have seen so many formerly strong, independent women laid low by marriage and motherhood.

*I have yet to see one single woman made stronger, more autonomous, more powerful, more self-confident or more independent by taking these steps. It is usually only when women come out of relationships, when their children have grown up and left home, that they can reclaim their own identity, their own power.*

But detaching mentally can be a slow and painful experience, particularly for women who have never really had any sense of separate identity in their lives. The only way to begin detaching is to try and gain the confidence to say 'I', to make your own decisions, even if these seem pathetically small at first, and then gradually becoming able to make larger ones. Women who feel they need to gain confidence even before taking the first timid steps to independence may find a local consciousness-raising (CR) group or assertiveness classes helpful.

The problem for so many women, says Janice Raymond (see chapter 2), is that they sit around waiting for life to happen to them, rather than taking the initiative. It can be extremely hard to make life happen when you have been used to sitting on the sidelines, having your decisions made for you, and have taken the 'supportive' rather than the leading role. But more women are doing it all the time and gradually, there are more role models becoming available. More women all the time are gaining the courage to end stifling and stultifying relationships, and strike out on their own.

The indications are that women who have divorced, who have become single, almost never regret it later. A survey of the careers of 500 divorced and separated men and women carried out in both Britain and America discovered that more than half of the women had increased their professional achievements after divorce, with 25 per cent reporting a decrease. The survey, conducted by Excel International, also found that women reported increased motivation and personal fulfilment after divorce.

One of the interviewees, Jackie, an estate agent, said: 'I've become much more assertive, much more my own person since getting divorced. Everybody who gets divorced has to take a long hard look at themselves. You can gain confidence from knowing that you are who you are, the kind of confidence that allows you to be assertive without being aggressive.'

Most women who responded to the survey said that they would never allow themselves to be so dependent as they had been before the divorce. 'For women, the marital home is often just a round of drudgery which they could do better without,' said one respondent.

Being single means you have to take the initiative all the time and while this is scary, it is also exciting. Very many women have absolutely no experience at all of being single until their relationships break up – and then they can be terrified of facing the world alone. They are suddenly thrust into an unfamiliar world, being a single in what seems like a world full of couples.

Sandra S. Kahn, author of *The Ex-Wife Syndrome*, says that many ex-wives, however old they may be, are like frightened children out there by themselves. They are so full of self-doubt they do not see how they can possibly manage on their own. The emotional experience of not having one other person to provide comfort, security and stimulation – however illusory these may be – is fearful indeed. But Kahn reminds us that on the whole, the sense of loss comes from the lack of attachment, rather than genuine devoted love for the former partner. There is a fear of letting go of control of somebody else, a fear of becoming a complete individual, standing on one's own.

Kahn believes there are three main areas of fear for the newly-single woman:

How am I going to handle the finances?
How am I going to enter the social world?
How will I run a household all by myself?

But all these fears fall away one by one as you do them. In her book *Feel the Fear and Do it Anyway*, Susan Jeffers reminds us that the only way to face fears and overcome them is to do the thing you are frightened of – then the fear vanishes.

It is mainly fear which keeps women in the state of bondage known as marriage, mainly fear which makes mothers plan for and hope for their daughters' weddings, mainly fear that allows us to see divorce and separation as failure, and tying the knot with somebody else as an indication of 'happiness.' Only recently, in an interview with thrice-divorced actor Dudley Moore, the interviewer drew attention to how 'happiness' had always eluded him – as he kept divorcing his wives. If only we could stop believing that happiness lies in bondage to another person, we would all be emotionally far healthier. But people always want everybody else to validate what they have done by joining them in the same boat.

It does take courage to go it alone, but the rewards are so much greater than those of binding yourself to another. For centuries, women have felt they've *had* to be married, otherwise they weren't fulfilling their womanhood in some way. Now, increasingly, there are the chances for women to do their own thing, unhampered by dependants being always around them. As a woman you can care for and nurture yourself – the most important task that anybody can do.

# Special Difficulties for Men

Although men are popularly assumed to be more independent and autonomous than women, less clinging, it is a fact that men find divorce and separation far more traumatic than women do, on the whole. They find being single more difficult, in spite of being bigger earners.

The same survey which discovered that women do better

careerwise after divorce found the opposite for men – that their careers and promotion prospects tend to decrease on divorce or separation. It has also been found in a number of surveys that single men on the whole earn less and have worse health than married ones; the opposite is true of women.

So what does this tell us? It tells us, however much we might want to believe the opposite, that marriage is made for men, it enlarges them, provides a support system, gives them status and a little empire. So no wonder they often feel extremely adrift, as if their whole world has fallen apart, when they become single. No longer are they head of a household, with a wife and children all bearing their name; no longer are they in charge of a little unit. No longer are they getting their shirts washed, their meals cooked, the housework done, the children looked after. No longer are they taking psychic support from being in charge of a woman.

The sense of being adrift that a man commonly feels when his marriage or relationship ends is one of hurt ego, a profound sense of rejection (how could she reject *me*?) and hurt pride. He is no longer successful as a man, if he can't trap and keep a woman. (These ideas, often buried deep in the unconscious, remain however 'equal' modern marriages may seem. It's still usually a question of Mr and Mrs, with his name in the telephone book and on the electricity bills.)

For many men, their 'freedom' may seem a small price to pay because as far as they were concerned, they were perfectly free anyway. Now, as increasingly happens, his wife has had the effrontery to leave him, taking, as often as not, a huge slice of the family assets that he had provided, and leaving him with practically nothing.

Perceived loss of status is no small thing for the average man, and the temptation for many when one relationship ends is to try and start another immediately. The problem nowadays for many middle-aged men, especially if they have lost money and property following divorce, and are having to pay alimony or child maintenance into the bargain, is that they are no longer the attractive prospects they may once have been. Many discover that they cannot sustain long-term relationships. And if they go for much younger women, as many do, they often find the woman wants to start a family, which the middle-aged man may be reluctant to do all over again. Newly-single men go for younger women not because younger women are intrinsically more attractive, but because they are possibly more easily impressed – they may not have heard all the jokes before.

A single man often feels: who am I, what am I, without a woman in tow? If I am alone, a single man may think, I am nobody. If there is nobody to look up to me, nobody to praise and worship and look after me, I'll hardly know whether or not I exist.

But it is ultimately a mistake to imagine that you can get a genuine sense of status from trying to lord it over other people. For centuries, men in the West have been able to terrorize women, one way and another and keep them in submission. Now it is getting increasingly difficult, and men are left wondering what their role is, what is their purpose in life. The answer is, of course, that it is the same as women's: to discover themselves, to grow personally, to be strong and autonomous, not at the expense of belittling everybody else, but out of a genuine sense of self-worth.

Now that ever more men are having no choice but to become single, a huge amount of reappraisal is becoming necessary. It may be important to mourn the loss of the old relationship, not stay mentally and emotionally glued to it, so that you can free yourself for the future. Anger and bitterness may be natural, but they will not contribute towards personal growth.

Many women, and possibly even more men, are nervous of embarking on a journey of self-discovery, in case they don't like what they find. But you'll never like yourself anyway until you make this journey.

Men, like women, have to realize that they are complete people in their own right. They do not need the appendage of a domestic slave, a fashion accessory, or a yes-woman – or should not – in order to feel somebody.

If you have been used to a relationship where you have been the boss, the provider, the kingpin, learning to be single can be hard. But as more and more women are taking the plunge into singlehood, men will have no choice but to follow, and in the future there will inevitably be many more single men.

One of the hardest things is dispelling the idea that you have a right to be looked after, and that you can't cope very well on your own. On the whole, men do not have the same problems as some women as regarding the single state as one of waiting, of being in limbo. They tend to be capable of getting on with their lives in the meantime.

Possibly the most difficult thing for the majority of men to accept about being single is that there may not be a regular sexual partner. But then, if you like variety, this may be a blessing rather than a handicap.

Think of the positive aspects of being single – nobody to nag at you to mow the lawn, drive the car somewhere, go with them to the supermarket, tidy up your clothes, put on records you don't like. You can take up your hobbies again, renew contact with your former friends. You can, for the first time in your life, find out who you are – and possibly be pleasantly surprised at the discovery.

# Enjoying Your Own Company

The whole point about enjoying your own company is that you have to feel that you, and you alone, are worth making an effort for.

It's most important to make a harmonious nest for yourself, one that works for you. If your flat or house or bedsitter is frankly a dump, because that's all you can afford, or because you don't know how to undump it, buy a copy of Barty Phillips' *Doing up a Dump* for cheap and cheerful ways of turning even the most unpromising rooms into a cosy home.

Once you have an attractive home to live in, you will automatically start feeling better about yourself. Put some individual touches here and there, your own paintings, pictures, photos – don't leave acres of bare walls. Plants and flowers are very important, so take the trouble to make sure you always have some fresh greenery in your home.

Although single people often have a much more exciting social life than couples, the fact is that you are as a single person inevitably going to spend some time on your own. Saturday nights, Sunday mornings, when you get home from work, are all times when you are likely to be alone. You will come home to an empty house, and it may be cold and unwelcoming at times, especially if you haven't made the bed or done the washing up.

The thing is not to be afraid of being alone, feeling lonely. The good thing about being alone on Sunday morning, for example, is that you can luxuriate in bed and get up when you want to.

Try to welcome feeling lonely, because it means that at least you are feeling. It is possible to become so anaesthetized by relationships that you have forgotten how to feel. Susan Jeffers says that many of us are so very afraid of being lonely that we drown out these emotions as they arise, and devise all kinds of escape routes for ourselves. We can get so caught up in activities that we don't have time to think and just be.

The reason so many of us feel lonely when we are alone is because we have not made the effort to connect properly with other people. When in a relationship, we can imagine that all our companionship needs will be taken care of in the one relationship, and we can forget how to make friends, to have proper companions.

The usual agony-aunt advice about being alone is: join a club where you can meet like-minded people. Not everything will work, and some clubs may make you feel lonelier than before, so it's not an automatic solution. My own feeling that the best way to get over feelings of loneliness is to make yourself useful in some capacity – offer to work for a charity, to help out, to do some kind of voluntary work. That way you will soon make friends, and soon get a 'feel' for who are your sort of people.

Susan Jeffers feels that loneliness is above all the result of a closed heart. We are lonely when we fear being hurt, or rejected or judged. We cannot feel empathy for other people, and so we remain in our own closed world.

It is only when the barriers start to break down that we can feel truly connected with other people. And once this happens, we will cease to feel lonely, even though we may be spending far more time alone than before.

For many people, relationships mask the fact that they are basically lonely, and this is a major reason why we fear to leave them. When we are in an exclusive relationship, in a sense it doesn't matter much whether we have friends, connect, whether we have hobbies. It is only once we are on our own that these lacks can become apparent.

It is only by facing our own loneliness that we can understand at last what we want, who we are, what we must do with our lives. Susan Jeffers writes:

*Loneliness can be beautiful when it moves us to new heights of awareness, when it pulls us forward to learn, seek and grow. As long as we use it as a tool for self-discovery, loneliness has magical results. It is a call forward and we should not be upset at its presence in our lives. We should just heed the call and ask ourselves how we can move forward in wholeness and love. There is nothing wrong with us when we feel our loneliness – it does not mean we are misfits or losers.*

Nowadays, it's so common to feel there is something wrong with us if we are lonely, and that if we spend too much time alone, we may well go mad. The fact is, most newly-single people discover that they are alone, or feel lonely, only for a very short time while they are getting used to their new state. It feels strange at first not to be part of a couple, and of course it takes getting used to. But how few people would swap it for cosy coupledom once they have got used to the feeling of freedom, have gone with the loneliness and discovered how very rich life can be when there is not just one other person to please and consider all the time.

As each 'alone' hurdle is crossed, you will feel a terrific sense of achievement and power – as if you have come up to breathe fresh air after being underground for years.

The main reason single people (or anyone at all) can feel lonely is because we are all so terrified of rejection and tend to think: if this person really liked me, they'd invite me to their place. But the fact is that most people are only going to invite you once or twice before they expect some reciprocal arrangement. Not having the confidence to take the initial step is part of the 'victim' mentality, which will never go away unless you address it.

Don't ever worry about not being able to afford to reciprocate invitations. People newly on their own are often poor, and it's quite in order to ask people to bring a contribution. Nobody will mind, nobody will condemn you for not having enough money – only for never inviting them round or being the one to suggest things.

It doesn't cost anything to go for a long walk – and this can be one of the most enjoyable ways of passing time with friends. It can also be extremely therapeutic.

It's once you have learned to be alone, once it starts to feel natural, that you will enjoy being single. You can't ever expect life to happen to you – you have to make it happen.

# 6

# Specific Problem Areas

here is no doubt that in many ways, life is easier if you're part of a couple. The whole of society today is geared towards couples, and continues to treat single people as oddities, untidy extras. This is how it has happened. Until the mid-nineteenth century, a woman disappeared completely on marriage. She forfeited her identity and her name – not only her surname but her first name as well, becoming Mrs John Smith. She was not allowed to own property, to pay taxes, to keep any money she did earn. Everything, including her body and her children, belonged to her husband and she had no status whatever in law. In fact, the law gave married women no rights at all. She became in every sense of the term, 'one flesh' with her husband.

Then came the suffragettes and other militant feminists who campaigned for women's rights. Throughout this century, married women have gradually accrued ever more legal rights, so that they can now pay their own taxes, buy and own property in their own names, and keep the money they earn. In many important ways, they are treated more and more as single women, and this has prompted diehards to mourn that separate taxation and so on is undermining the institution of marriage.

But in their new eagerness to treat married women as proper people, banks, tax officials and other financial institutions have, unwittingly, promoted the idea of the couple above everything. Most bank accounts and mortgages are now in joint names, whereas at one time, most were for men only. By increasingly targeting married women as people in their own right, advertisers have promoted the idea of the couple as the only unit that really counts. This is, of course, an improvement on the days when married women simply disappeared for ever, but it has meant that single people are increasingly feeling discriminated against.

For instance, there are family rail discount cards; families and couples get better deals on holidays than single people; most charities, museums, and societies have 'couple' memberships, which are cheaper than two single ones. The paradox is that, by allowing that married women now exist as people, everything is now geared and targeted to heterosexual couples. This means that single people can feel distinctly odd as they try to book a holiday, stay in a hotel, or join a club, and then find they have to pay far more than a couple of people who are joined together.

No wonder single people can feel nowadays as if the dice are loaded against them. It can be more difficult in some ways to go it alone – but don't be tempted to enter a relationship just because you feel it might make life easier. All the practicalities of being single can be coped with –

once you have become, as we discussed in the previous chapter, mentally single.

# Managing Money

Possibly the biggest problem area for most newly-single people is money, having one income instead of two, and trying to make it do exactly the same work. It can be hard to know how to manage if you're a man who now has to pay out regular maintenance, the previous mortgage and is reduced to living in a bedsitter, as often happens these days, or a woman who has not earned regular money for many years. You are no longer propping each other up; you have to manage somehow on your own, and nobody is ever going to come and take money worries away from you.

The big questions for most people living on their own are: how do I get more money? How do I get enough? There are no easy answers, but the worst thing you can do is to pretend that money worries will just go away of their own accord.

The first thing is to face them. Very many people can't face money matters at all, and just pray there will be enough to cover the bills. This can lead to desperate over-spending or equally desperate hoarding. The second thing to realize is that living well doesn't have to cost all that much – although it will probably take some adjustment.

You have to work out your own attitude to money, and if you have merged finances in a previous relationship, this may be difficult to know at first. Are you basically a risk-taker or a conserver? Careful or prodigal? Do you want to be employed or self-employed? There is some evidence to suggest that single people tend to be self-employed more frequently than those in partnerships.

Financial advisor Lorna Galbraith-Ryan believes that some kind of management system for finances is essential, even if you've got hardly any spare cash. You should always keep your bank statements in numerical order, after checking them for accuracy; make notes on credit card statements as to when you paid and how much; be able to find your tax records; and keep copies of all correspondence relating to finances.

Your motto should always be, she suggests: live for today and plan for tomorrow.

You should force yourself to keep a weekly budget, and try to stick to it. (Budgets are a bit like slimming diets – people cheat all the time.) Then get into the habit of reading all your bank statements and checking them very carefully.

Do not enter into any hire-purchase, credit-card or other financial arrangements until you are absolutely certain of what you are doing, what the interest payments will be, and how you are going to pay them back. If you get into a real mess, contact your local Citizen's Advice Bureau, many of which now have special debt counsellors who can advise people on how best to manage their finances. It is a good idea to use the old-fashioned method of saving up for things before you buy them, rather than thinking you must have this or that *now*. For example, as a single person you may well be able to do without a car. Although I had access to a car from the age of 17, soon after I became single, I felt I could not afford to run or own one. So I sold it, and managed for nearly three years without one. In that time I saved – or at least, didn't spend – a considerable amount of money, enabling me to finish off the house repairs, which were at the time more important to me.

You will find that you can live far more cheaply than you may have imagined. You will also most probably discover that your finances soon improve, and that managing on your own seems the most natural thing in the world.

American writer Louise L. Hay, a member of the Science of Mind religious movement, feels that the way to have plenty of money is to believe that there is always enough available in the universe, and that your needs will be provided. If you sincerely believe this, she says, you will never be poor. You owe it to yourself to be well housed, well dressed, well fed and nourished – and you have to realize that nobody but you can provide these things.

Ernest Holmes, the founder of Science of Mind, taught that everybody's financial prosperity already existed, and that all you have to do is to see it and accept it. I'm not sure whether I go along with this completely, but it is a fact that if you believe you deserve to be prosperous, if you are generous and giving in nature, then riches will return to you.

The way to become prosperous as a single person is to have a goal, and then steadfastly aim at it. Tim, a piano teacher, could not seem to make ends meet. He found it difficult to charge enough money for lessons, even though he was good at his job. He also could not seem to cope with schools and institutions, where he could have got a lot of work. As a result, he was always poor, always on his beam ends.

Then a very wise old lady said that he should aim at having £500 in the bank. Previously, Tim had never had anything in the bank at all, in fact he was always in arrears. But this goal enabled him to charge proper rates, and to get more pupils. When he had the £500, the same old lady said: 'Now make it a thousand.' When he had £1000, he felt rich for the first time in his life.

Somebody who was impressed with his high standards of teaching gave Tim the use of a house he owned at a low rent, and Tim made it the basis of a small music centre. Previously, as he had lived in digs, he had to travel to his pupils' homes – now they came to him.

Today Tim is not rich, but neither is he poor. He runs a car, he makes ends meet, and his musical career is thriving. He said: 'It can be summed up in just one word: self-respect.'

Often, single people do not have much respect for themselves, believing that they don't count, that they aren't as important as couples and families. The sense of self-esteem, a theme which runs through the whole of this book, can be very low if you are newly single, or if you feel you ought to have attracted a mate but haven't managed it.

It's when you start to feel 'I don't matter' that your finances tend to get into difficulties. Once you can persuade yourself that you do matter, then you can start to look at ways to attract more money to you – possibly by taking a night course, by looking for a new job and not to be over-concerned with job security (nowadays there is simply no such thing).

If you have recently come out of a long relationship, try not to feel bitter that your former partner may have come off better than you. Just work with the assets you have. Expect that it will be tough at first, simply because disentangling joint financial matters is a highly emotive activity, as well as possibly being extremely difficult.

It may not be possible for you to buy a house or flat, even if as a couple you owned the family home, because your partner may have kept it. Nowadays, with housing being a far less good investment than formerly, renting is often a good idea, especially at first. It means you are more flexible, and if you have a little bit of capital, it can start to earn interest while you are deciding what to do.

There is also the fact that splitting up itself will cost money. This is not a book on how to split up and survive financially – there are a number of those already on the market – but divorces, lawyers, conciliation experts, marriage guidance counsellors, and bottles of wine shared with friends whose shoulders you cry on, all add up.

Paul, in the case history in chapter 3, estimated that he and his ex-wife spent around £3000 each on lawyers – money neither of them could easily afford, and it didn't make the divorce any more amicable. If you have assets to divide, try to work out how this can be done to save money going unnecessarily down the drain.

Many – possibly most – of us have some kind of block about money, which is not easy to overcome. Being single forces you to deal with your finances, to live within your income, because there is no other source of cash available, and to try and find ways of improving your income once you have established your new lifestyle.

It may be that you will want to share with somebody, to cut costs. This arrangement can work, so long as you can respect each other's privacy and so long as neither of you is tied up in some hard-to-reverse arrangement, such as a joint mortgage. If you think you might like to share a house, perhaps you could give it a trial first, to see whether it works out. Living with somebody on a shared basis is very different from living with a partner.

If you are single with children, never be too proud to accept maintenance for the children from your ex. Although non-custodial parents – usually fathers – are often blamed for not paying maintenance, there is also the fact that exes often feel so bitter that they hate the thought of being 'beholden.' But although you may not want to accept the previous partner's money for yourself, do not refuse it for your children. Apart from anything else, it will make both the non-custodial parent and the children still feel connected.

# Coping with Children

It's a fact of life that very many single people these days are parents. As they struggle to bring up their children, they keep reading reports saying that children from 'broken homes' do worse at school, have a greater tendency to become delinquent than children from two-parent homes, that they are poorer, and they are discriminated against.

For this reason, single parents often feel they ought to remarry, to make things look more normal. *Don't do it* – at least, not 'for the sake of the children'. I have never met a child who relishes the prospect of an interloper coming into the house and being given authority. All the indications are that children are happier being with one parent than with one parent plus a stepmother or father, who then claims so much of the 'real' parent's attention. At least with a sole parent, the children know that they are important.

Of course, life can be hard for single parents – you've got the children day in, day out without any let-up, or anybody else to share day-to-day decisions such as how late the children should stay out, how much pocket money they should have, what kind of clothes they should wear, and so on.

One thing single parents should not worry about is that their children will automatically fare worse than children with two parents. In her book *Men: The Darker Continent* psychologist Heather Formaini says that children of single parents frequently do not correspond psychologically to children who live with two parents – they are often emotionally much healthier. This may be because there is no conflict between parents – something children pick up from a very early age, even if they don't articulate it – and because mothers (90 per cent of single parents are female) say they find it easier being with children on their own without a man making extra demands.

In fact, although single parents are supposed to have such a struggle, the facts are, as is frequently the case, the very opposite of what we have been led to believe. Very many women feel divided between the claims of their children and the claims of their husbands, not knowing which should come first. This was particularly noticeable during the days of British rule in India, when mothers of even quite young children would leave them with virtual strangers for years on end while they accompanied their husbands as Memsahibs. Even now, wives of servicemen, diplomats and international businessmen will put their seven-year old children in boarding schools so that they can be with their husbands. When there is no husband or man around, then this conflict simply doesn't arise – the children come first.

Children of single parents often do extremely well at school and professionally in later life for the simple reason that they receive more attention from the one parent than they would if that parent was trying to have a 'fulfilling' relationship with a spouse or partner. The only real danger for single parents is if they start trying to treat their children as mini-adults and confidants. Children are children, they are not equals and they are not friends. They do not want to hear about your sex life, and they certainly do not want to hear you running down the absent parent.

Heather Formaini adds that another advantage of being brought up by a single mother is that children do not get the same sense of the inferiority of their mothers, which can come directly from the father, if he is the major earner, if mother defers to him, and so on.

As Formaini points out, the biggest difficulty for single parents is financial – and it's hard to see how that will change in the future. Even single fathers are often on social security, as they have not been able to find a way to combine work and family responsibilities.

Martin became a single father when his wife left him with two small children and ran away with her lover. There has been no contact since. As the children were then aged three and five, Martin gave up his job as a social worker to look after them full-time. But he did it all very methodically. He put ads in local papers and newsagents to contact other single fathers in his area, and between them they devised a plan of action which would enable the children to make friends, and give all of the men some spare time. By dividing childcare, and joining forces to buy food and supplies in bulk, Martin managed very well.

When his younger son started school, he went back to work part time and when he was nine, began a full-time job. 'We three "men" grew up very happily together,' he said. 'I found household tasks extremely simple, to my surprise, and the only real problem was making friends with single mothers, as it would be easy to get the wrong idea.

'But with other single fathers, we went on all kinds of adventures, and became extremely self-sufficient.' Martin's sons, Toby and Alex, are now 17 and 19 and every girl's dream. 'They can cook, wash up, look after themselves – they've had to. And as Alex is at Cambridge and Toby starts art college next year, they certainly haven't missed out academically.'

Single parents are common nowadays, and there are many organizations, such as the well-established Gingerbread, which can help with social life, arranging childcare and holidays, and managing finances.

Ever more women are now deciding to have children without a permanent partner anyway – and there is no indication that these very wanted and loved children suffer in any way. Most of the former stigma attached to illegitimacy has now vanished, and children from one-parent homes are as accepted in society and in school as children from two-parent homes. Indeed, in secondary schools it is becoming the exception, rather than the norm, to have two original parents who are still married to one another.

Women who do not wish to marry often ask themselves whether it would be fair to have a child without a man – fair to the child, that is. The story of explorer and writer Dervla

Murphy illustrates what a wonderful life a child can have with one unusual parent. Dervla had to leave school at the age of 14 to look after her invalid mother. She did not become free until she was in her thirties, when her mother died. After bicycling round India, and taking a number of other long-distance trips, she decided at the age of 36 that she wanted to have a child, although the idea of marriage was hateful to her.

She was having a close relationship with a man at the time, and soon conceived. She gave up travelling until her daughter Rachel was five, supporting herself by writing. But then she took her daughter to India and later, to Peru. Rachel, now in her twenties, has been all over the world with her mother, and features in many of Dervla's books.

Dervla decided to send Rachel to a coed boarding school, Millfield, both to give herself time to write and so that Rachel would mix with members of the opposite sex. Dervla has never been financially supported by a man, and there is no indication that Rachel has 'suffered' in any way.

As a single parent, you can give more time to your children, even if you are working full time. The presence of another biological parent does not mean happiness at all – only that the situation may look more 'normal' to outsiders. Financial problems can often be eased by sharing, by combining with others to go to wholesale supermarkets and taking advantage of bulk offers.

Being a single parent does not mean you have to be lonely – just that, as with any other kind of single life, you may have to work harder to get it all together. It may not 'just happen'.

# Holidays

Holidays are often a problem area for single people, whether or not they have children. The problem is more easily solved if you do have children, as there are so many cheap holidays where you can take them these days, and where they can have a wonderful time.

The real difficulty comes with lone holidays, especially when you have been used to being one of a partnership, and when you find you have to pay twice as much for everything, at the same time as possibly having less money to spend. (That's another thing about the single life nowadays – single people, who very often have less disposable cash than each member of a couple, find they have to pay much more for everything.)

When newly single, it may be an idea to try and find another single friend with whom to go on holiday. This is what I did when recently separated. I travelled to India and went on a Himalayan trek with a friend who had also recently divorced. We wondered whether we would be able to get on together for a month under difficult conditions and discovered, to our delight, that we got on far better than we had with our respective spouses when we had tried adventure holidays. Although there was companionship, there was not the closeness and the conflict which often happens when married people go on holiday together. In fact, family holidays cause more squabbles and rows than almost any other shared activity.

If you can't find a friend, it's as well to pick an activity holiday, something where you will meet other singles, and where you don't feel left out if you're not a couple. I have been on tennis holidays, retreats, self-discovery weeks, all by myself – holidays that would probably not have been possible as a 'double'. I have met lots of new people, something else that you don't tend to do on a couple or family holiday. Dervla Murphy has pointed out that you never really see anything of the country or get to know its people when you are travelling with a spouse or partner, as you form a little sealed unit that nobody likes to disturb. I would say that my best and most enjoyable holidays are those where I've been alone. It's perfectly possible and extremely worthwhile. Nobody should ever be afraid of going on holiday alone, unless it is to lie on a beach for two weeks, when you may find it very lonely being surrounded by couples and families.

Holiday companies offering 'singles' holidays are usually for the purpose of meeting up with a dashing young person of the opposite sex, although in reality this rarely happens. I would strongly advise against special singles holidays, which tend to be an expensive waste of time, where the emphasis is on having 'fun' – and where often, you don't have fun at all. If you don't meet somebody you are liable to be disappointed, and if you do, they may well seem far more attractive than they really are simply because you are meeting them out of context.

Activity or 'hobby' holidays are the thing for single people, as you are liable to meet people who share your interests, and with whom you can talk. Skiing, for example, is perfectly possible on your own, as après-ski is always a very easy time to meet new people and share experiences. Also, skiing holidays are usually so tiring that you won't probably want to be up late at night. Painting and pottery holidays are also enjoyable if you already have some skills in this direction or would like to learn them, and, for older people, cultural holidays can be very rewarding. There are pilgrimages available, treks, small guided tours, walking holidays, holidays for women only – nowadays the choice is vast.

Rachel Lever runs *The Henhouse*, a women-only conference and holiday centre in the north of Lincolnshire. Her idea was to start a hotel for women which would be comfortable, stylish and inexpensive, and the venture has proved very successful. Single women of all ages – and even some married ones who are somewhat tired of their relationships – go to the hotel to relax with women only (the domestic staff are all female, as are even the cats), and to escape the attentions of the opposite sex. Women-only and other specialist hotels and holiday centres are now catering more and more for the single person who wants an active, purposeful social life and does not want to pretend he or she is one of a couple.

Health farms are expensive, but places where you will always find plenty of other single people, there to try and reduce stress and recharge the batteries. Most people, even if they are married or in partnerships, go to health farms alone. You can also go on fasting weekends by yourself – you'll have plenty to talk about, with everybody suffering equally.

If you are single, don't imagine you have to give up on enjoyable holidays. The chances are that you just have to rethink a little what you would like to gain from a holiday – relaxation, sun, improving your skill in a hobby, sport or interest, personal growth, strenuous physical activity, meeting people or largely being alone. Once you are clear in your head about what you want, then you will find no shortage of choices.

## Sex and Relationships

I've left this until last because it is the most difficult. The problem for most single people is not so much finding sexual partners – anybody who really wants sex will discover that this is easy enough – but knowing what they want out of a relationship, whether they are looking for somebody permanent, whether they simply want companionship, and what they should do if casual relationships threaten to turn into something more serious.

There is also the difficulty of maintaining friendships with the opposite sex without the sexual element.

The solution, as with holidays, is to be absolutely clear in your head what you want – and then the rest will follow. If you, as a newly-single person, know that under any circumstances you do not want to get married again, then you have to make this clear from your attitude at the start. Few single people, unless they are hard-line separatist feminists or gays, want to lead the rest of their lives without any contact whatever with the opposite sex.

Some men believe it is actually impossible to have a close friendship with a woman, especially if she is an attractive woman, without this turning into physical intimacy and bed. It is certainly more difficult than to have a close relationship with a member of your own sex, as there is, very often, a deep attraction to the opposite, and when both partners are free, there seems nothing wrong with it.

*151*

I'm not saying necessarily that there is anything wrong, but it is a fact that sex always fundamentally changes the nature of any relationship. It is no longer a platonic friendship, for a start, and the danger is that once you have a sexual relationship with somebody, you may start believing you have claims on them, and them on you. The sense of ownership, of possession, quickly creeps in when the relationship turns sexual. Then it is all too easy to get into the habit of saying 'we', of being a couple once more.

Some single people wonder what they will do with their sex drive, when there is no regular partner available. But this is much like anything else – the sense of frustration, the perceived need for physical intimacy, lasts for only a short time before it begins to recede. The desire for intimacy will not live for long in the abstract, but it can be kindled almost ad infinitum when opportunity presents itself.

Another problem with a sexual relationship is the possibility that both people may not want the same thing from the affair – one may not want commitment, while the other may be pressing for something more exclusive, more permanent.

Certainly, you do not have to allow anybody to have a sexual relationship with you if you are sure this isn't what you want, so never be afraid to say no at the end of an evening, even a 'romantic' one.

The thing about affairs is that they can be extremely exciting, possibly the most exciting things that can happen to us. But even with the most wonderful person in the universe, the excitement soon palls and the relationship becomes ordinary. You get used to it.

Very often, women who have come out of a long-term

relationship feel they want at least a rest from sexual involvement until they have sorted themselves out and got their lives back together again. Never be in too much of a hurry to start up a sexual relationship and, given the nature of the sex drive, always ask yourself whether you want to activate your sexuality with this particular person. Sex has a peculiar way of binding people to each other – even if they're not all that much in love, and particularly if they're feeling vulnerable.

What about if you do fall in love? I would say that it is easy to fall in love when you are newly single, simply because you have not got used to being on your own, and because the habit of bonding with another person remains very strong. Although it doesn't seem as though there's much you can do about it, at least wait to see if the passion lasts before making any serious life changes. Try and live on your own for a bit first, before plunging into a new relationship. Statistically speaking, relationships which happen on the rebound after long-married people get divorced, are extremely short-lived.

Before tying yourself up in any irrevocable way with somebody else, get used to being single, to being on your own, and discovering who you are. You may find that, as you remove yourself from your previous kind of life, your tastes have changed and that you now want quite different relationships from the ones you had before.

If you plunge too early into a mad round of sex and casual affairs, you might just be substituting one sedative for another. Men often embark on a heady series of affairs when relationships end, believing that they are now free and can do as they like. But the risk is that addiction to short-lived intense relationships will develop, and this of course will bring stress and ultimate unhappiness.

Never have sex with somebody because you feel lonely, or as a way of trying to connect to other people. It doesn't work – and you will end up feeling used, lonely and more disconnected than before.

The best advice for the newly single is to tread very carefully at first and make sure you offer only friendship, nothing more, until you are certain whether you want something more committed, more intimate. Don't forget that you are free now, and nobody has any claims on you at all. It can be very tempting for the newly single to contact old flames, to see if there is still any spark going. It is actually quite common for people to form new relationships and even marry old flames, people they may have lost touch with for 20 years or more. On the one hand, if it didn't work then it's unlikely to work now; on the other, here is somebody you don't have to go through all the hassle of getting to know, as you know them already. They know your past history, knew you when you were younger. For them, you were not always the age you are now. And nowadays, they too might well be single again – so all the dangers are there.

There is nothing inherently wrong about contacting former lovers and offering friendship. After all, if you are now both free you may well be able to strike up a good relationship in a more mature way. I would say that it is far easier to strike up a friendship with an old flame, particularly if in the past you have had a sexual relationship, and remain friends with no strings attached. One of the pleasanter aspects for me of becoming single is that I have been able to renew contact with several old flames and establish non-sexual but close friendships.

However, difficulties can arise for single people when there are vastly different income levels – and these days, it's not always the man who has most money. Kim had been single for several years when she re-met Mike, to whom she had been engaged briefly at university. Kim had a highly glamorous and well-paid job as a television presenter. Mike, who had been divorced fairly recently, had no money at all as he was having to pay maintenance and in any case, was not earning much from his job as a librarian.

For many years, Kim had been used to the high life. She had always been fond of Mike, so she invited him out to dinner, back to her place for champagne and once or twice to the theatre. For a time, it was fun getting to know Mike again and catching up on their adult lives. But it soon became very one-sided. Mike simply could not afford to reciprocate the arrangements and before long, the relationship foundered. It is sad, maybe, that relationships will often fail when there are great disparities in income, but the point is, you are starting out with enormous inequality, and if you want an equal relationship, then the money aspect can be difficult to solve. Rich men don't want to take out poor single women for long – unless perhaps they are extremely young. But even then, they will soon come to demand a return on their investment.

Many men feel that unless the relationship is going to lead somewhere – i.e. in bed – there is not a lot of point in them taking single women out to lunch, dinner, the theatre. When you are single, close relationships, either with the opposite or the same sex, will very much depend on similarity of income. Otherwise, the difficulties can be almost insurmountable. But apart from the money aspect, no relationship can work if it becomes all too obviously one-sided. For single people's relationships and affairs to work, there must be complete reciprocity in every way. Otherwise one partner will soon feel used, underappreciated, exploited and so on. The days when men were glad to take women out endlessly, paying for everything, are over – and if, as is so often the case these days, the man is still paying out for the previous relationship, he won't have the money either.

As a single woman, you should not expect to be 'taken' out all the time, or paid for. You are equal now. If you go away with a new lover to a hotel for the weekend, pay your share. Or, he pays for one weekend and you pay for the next. If you can't pay, don't go – it will put you in an inferior position. The same applies to single men.

A number of American books for divorced and separated people address the problem of dating again, when you may not have done this for very many years. I would say it's far more important to get to know yourself, to settle into your new life and try not to worry about 'dating' until you feel serene and confident by yourself. Otherwise, you will simply attach yourself to another weak, vulnerable, possibly bitter person – and no good relationship can ever come out of that.

In the meantime, offer friendship, take the initiative, phone people up and ask them out, or round to your place as friends, not prospective lovers or partners. If the relationship doesn't develop, it doesn't much matter, as you have got to know a new person and have lost nothing. If it seems to be turning into something more serious, monitor it carefully all the time so that at any stage you can pull back.

Never get sucked into a new relationship, and always ask yourself whether you really want to be tied up again after becoming free.

The best attitude to have is one of lightness and detachment. See how you get on, see how comfortable you feel – and if people start to irritate you, you don't have to continue the friendship. There should be no pressure on you to form exclusive relationships, to feel dragooned into going out with somebody simply because you are both free, and single.

The thing to realize is that there is no inherent advantage in having somebody to go out with, somebody to sleep with – having exclusive relationships can cause more problems than they solve, especially as you get older, more set in your ways, and less keen to compromise.

Being single is a time to reassess stereotypes, to build relationships on a different basis, and not to get sucked into yet another form of bondage. The chances are that the more you get to like yourself, and the more comfortable you become with your single state, the less you will want it disturbed by another marriage-type relationship. You can love people in a different way, without wanting to tie them to you, or you to them. You can love them and let them go – and retain your self-respect.

# 7
# The Way Forward

I t may seem that I have painted a very black picture of modern relationships, as dysfunctional, codependent, unhealthy partnerships which cannot truly satisfy either person.

But the fact is that when the heterosexual couple is seen by society as a virtually indivisible unit, and more viable and valid than singleness, as the absolute norm, and when no real sanction is given to any other kind of way of living in the world, this is bound to happen.

At the moment, all kinds of people get bound up into cosy couples, when this kind of existence may simply not be right for them.

And because we set so much store by intimate partnerships, because we have so very many expectations of them, of course there are going to be relationship difficulties, problems of identity, of self-esteem. Of course there are going to be wrong, disastrous couplings, of course people are going to become desperately disappointed with the outcome of what at first may have seemed wonderfully romantic. The gap between the powerful myth of lifelong intimate attachment, being all in all to one another, and the reality of the boredom, the disillusion, the disappointment as the years go by, has never been wider.

It's not just that we may so easily hitch ourselves to the 'wrong person' – it's a matter of whether such hitching can ever really be personally fulfilling and satisfying on a fundamental level.

We have taken on board the idea that the couple is a natural, God-given unit, a union made in heaven and the way things are meant to be. What we often don't appreciate is that tightly-sealed couples and nuclear families are extremely new in our history, dating back only a hundred years at most.

For most of history, people have lived in extended families and had far looser bonds to each other. Because there were so many more people around in each family and home to relate to, such intense, intimate bonds with one other person of the opposite sex simply did not develop. Also, there was a place for those who did not form partnerships, did not marry or reproduce – they could all be part of the family, and had their functions and were respected for it.

A visit to any traditional society still existing shows that this is still the case. There is virtually no such thing as 'romantic love', and the fierce attachment and addiction which people now have towards each other in the West, the way they feel crippled and rudderless if the partner dies or disappears, and the great insistence on sex as the most natural form of expression of affection, as absolutely central to the health and success of the partnership, simply does not exist.

How far it is 'natural' to want to form close ties with one other person and reproduce one's own kind is not known – humans are such diverse creatures, and have erected so many different types of civilization and society over the centuries, that it is impossible to say what is and is not natural.

All we can say is that, for whatever reasons, the unit of the closely-knit, exclusive, heterosexual couple simply does not work, and that it is never found in any traditional society.

This is mainly because the tightly-bound couple itself is isolating; it makes people withdraw from other contact and try to imagine that each can fully satisfy the other's needs – a patent impossibility. No one person can ever satisfy every aspect of ourselves, however talented, clever, rich or beautiful they may be. The closely-knit union of a man and a woman, held up as an ideal, is not so much bonding as bondage. In order to make it work, or to keep it together, there must be enormous compromises from one or both partners. It is simply not possible for two fully-functioning, whole people to be bound up for life, and to be eternally happy, in such a union.

Very often, it will be the weaker, more sensitive, or more dependent partner who makes the sacrifices, denies themselves. In the past, this has usually, although not always, been the woman, but as women become more financially independent, and consequently grow in assertiveness, it can easily be the man who compromises his career, plays second fiddle, walks a couple of steps behind.

Either way, if one partner is going to feel second rate, invisible, supernumerary, that is not a recipe for happiness. Coupledom elevates one partner: there is not usually room for two whole people. One will be centre stage while the other plays a bit part.

The few relationships which do appear to allow both partners equal freedom, equal space to develop their careers and personal fulfilment, can be considered marriages of convenience. The reason these relationships seem to work is because each party is relatively detached from the other. They are not 'in love', and they operate more as a business partnership than a closely-knit couple. Yet relationships of this type, the sort that actually can work, are not held up as the ideal: we prefer to hear about spouses and partners who are so 'devoted' to the other that they are prepared to give up everything to follow and serve them.

The reality is that underneath the apparent devotion lies an enormous amount of resentment, denial and pain – nobody really likes to come second, to be the consort, the invisible partner. As we now know, people who do devote themselves to others are more likely to be codependent – needy individuals with low self-esteem and no sense of identity – than emotionally healthy. They then pass this codependency down to their children, which can easily lead to alcoholism, sex addiction or other mind-altering substances and activities.

The more you 'devote' yourself to another person and deny your own needs, the further away you get from knowing and understanding your true self. It is my view that the elevation of the lovey-dovey couple at the expense of any other type of relationship has been responsible for most of society's present ills. The monogamous heterosexual couple, by and large, is the most dysfunctional unit on earth.

The fact is that almost everybody who tries to bond exclusively with one person of the opposite sex for life, excluding all others, will eventually have 'relationship problems' and will almost certainly also have sexual problems, when the sex has become boring or routine – as it inevitably will as time goes by.

But instead of accepting that of course people who try to intertwine so closely, to deny their individuality and character by trying to be like everybody else, will eventually have serious problems, we do our utmost to therapize them back into the unit. We are extremely reluctant to take on board the idea that the unit itself may be inherently unhealthy, that it is ultimately stifling, a burden to men and women alike.

We have 'family therapy', 'couples therapy' – all ultimately doomed to failure because the units themselves are sick, a product of an ailing rather than a healthy society.

The fact that there are a thousand and one books telling people how to have a good relationship, how to be intimate, how to bond for life, how to make love with just one person for ever and enjoy it, should give us the clue. It's like diet books. If diets worked, we would need only one book on the subject. Instead, because the promise that we can lose eight pounds in a week, or eat less for life and love it, is a false one, we have to have ever more books trying to convince us that there's some way of losing weight and keeping it off while eating all the foods you most enjoy. Similarly, it's a lie that we can remain bonded healthily to one other person for ever, that we can be in love for ever, or that sex with the same person can get better and better as the years go by. The reason we want to believe the fantasy is basically because we are too frightened to get to know ourselves.

The closer the relationship seems, the more devoted the couple are to each other, the more frightened they are of facing the world alone, of facing up to the reality of themselves.

It is enormous fear that makes us try to preserve marriages, to put 'work' and 'commitment' into them, and to pretend that there must somewhere be a magic formula for keeping us bound together. Nowadays, of course, we as a society have bought the lie that frequent, 'exciting' sex can be the magic glue that will bind us to partners who have long since ceased to arouse any real passion or excitement.

In the past, it was actual laws that stopped us from uncoupling. Most people today simply have no idea how very recent the present divorce laws are. Even in the 1950s and 60s, it was virtually impossible to get a divorce unless one party agreed to be the 'guilty' one, and arranged to have a private detective to catch him or her in bed with somebody else in a hotel room.

And in those days, divorced people, especially women, were looked down on as not quite respectable. Then, as now, it was seen as the woman's job to hold the family unit together, to preserve the little home, to pretend that everything was all right.

Although divorce and separation are so much easier these days, there is still the lingering feeling that it's a good thing to keep the relationship going, and people are still consumed with guilt if they don't manage it; they are made to feel failures, that the relationship has broken down, rather than that they have reclaimed their freedom. So, they go to Relate or other 'marriage guidance' counselling, they try to redefine the relationship, they may try to have affairs with other people, with the full consent of the other party, or live 'open' marriages, or enact 'sensate focus', where they try to pleasure each other anew without actual sex – any old rubbish just to keep it going. The truth is, it's doomed anyway when it gets to that point, and any attempts to inject life and vigour into the relationship will only ever be short-acting drugs.

The fact is that when one or both parties feel stifled within the relationship, as eventually one or the other will, it is effectively over. Nothing will ever bring back the honeymoon closeness, whatever therapy or sex sessions are recommended.

The truth is, there is no real point any more in the couple. In the days when we had to reproduce to survive, when women simply had no choice but to get married, and when family units were absolutely necessary for the continuance of an agrarian community and subsistence economy, things were very different. But what is happening now is that as the actual need to form these bonds gets ever more tenuous, the perceived need to tie ourselves to other people, people who can usually give us nothing, bring us no real or lasting happiness, because they are as flawed and inadequate as we are ourselves, grows ever stronger. Basically, it's happening because we are so terrified of being on our own, of facing the world as an independent, complete, fully-functioning and separate individual.

Having said all this, I do not dispute that couples, and couple life, can be fun. When my husband and myself were first married, we had an enormous amount of fun. We enjoyed discovering things together, we made friends with other like-minded couples, and would have parties and go on holiday together. I was never lonely, I was never alone.

It all felt very secure and there were certainly good times. But being in a couple wasn't enough of a sedative to stop me getting desperately depressed when I could not seem to get anywhere with my career, it did not ever make me feel happier or more contented with myself. Although I could lose myself to a certain extent within the unit, the anaesthetic was always threatening to wear off, and there was the ever-present threat that I would have to face myself one day.

Even the most loving partner cannot really protect you – my husband could do nothing to alleviate my disappointment when work went badly, he could do nothing to prevent me being hurt when bosses and colleagues shunned me, or when I was given the sack or made redundant. He could do nothing to make me feel happy with my body, my achievements, my life.

Nor could I do any of this for him. We simply did not believe each other's reassurances.

All of life's battles eventually have to be faced on our own. And however close and devoted a couple seem, there is never any guarantee that their attachment to one another will prevent them falling in love or having affairs with somebody else. In fact, latest estimates show that in around eight out of ten couples, one or both of the partners now have extra-marital affairs.

The pretty notion that the couple is an indivisible, secure unit is highly illusory, offering no genuine security, comfort or protection. Here are a few case histories which illustrate how illusory it can all be.

When she was 22, Susanna married a man seven years older who was already a successful businessman. He was tall, strong, well (or at least, expensively) educated, rich and good looking. He was also a very good earner, and his success in business enabled them to have homes in Switzerland, London and the country.

As the years went by, and they had four children, the relationship became ever more unequal. Susanna had not worked since getting married and had no idea how to earn her own living. She eventually felt they were not communicating, that Philip was bullying her and acting superior, and she wanted to leave him – but how could she? She had no money of her own, had always been used to an expensive lifestyle and employed nannies, au pairs, cleaners and cooks. She had 'everything' – but she became ever more unhappy.

Because there seemed to be so much to lose, Susanna and Philip went to marriage guidance to try and patch up their relationship. It appeared to work for a bit, and then suddenly Philip's business crashed. He had a severe nervous breakdown, and has now not worked for several years. The money is all dwindling away – and Susanna feels horribly cheated. This tall, handsome, rich and successful man has let her down.

Susanna, now in her forties, is one of the many women who married men they thought would be good providers – and have seen how this has not proved to be the case.

When Margot married Tristan he was only twenty, but he had very big ideas about making a fortune and having a flat in every major city in the world. He was intelligent, confident and very, very ambitious.

He worked hard to qualify as an accountant, and for a time was enormously successful, almost a millionaire. Margot lived the life of Riley with fur coats, sports cars and beautiful homes. She did not work. Then Tristan was caught embezzling funds, and staged a disappearance. He is now living in semi-hiding, on very little money, and does not expect to work again. He and Margot are divorced, she has had to try and find a job – they never had children – and she wonders whatever happened to bring her such bad luck.

Aileen was a struggling actress when she married Geoff, a quantity surveyor. She thought that as he had a steady job, he would be able to give her security while she got her career off the ground. For a time, as a young, pert comedy actress, she was quite successful, but then she hit her thirties, and the parts started to fall off. They had two sons, both at private schools.

Then Geoff had a series of disasters. He was made redundant from the firm where he had worked for more than 10 years, and he set up on his own. That did not work out at all, and he simply could not make a go of it. Meanwhile, there were the school fees to pay. Aileen had to try to take over as breadwinner, knowing she could no longer rely on Geoff.

Perhaps nowadays fewer women would marry for money or security – but the habit dies hard. Women, as Colette Dowling observed in her perceptive *The Cinderella Complex*, are deeply conditioned to want a Prince Charming, and will try to fashion such a being from very unpromising material.

Men also can believe they are getting some kind of security from marriage or a lasting partnership, and nowadays, they are increasingly looking for women to marry who themselves have safe, steady jobs. A conversation I overheard on the train was a significant sign of the times. Two young men were commuting to work. The first one said: 'I'd like to buy a house, but I can't afford a mortgage.'

The second young man said: 'You ought to get married, then you'll have two incomes.'

First young man: 'But my girlfriend's a freelance graphic

designer. She doesn't have a reliable income.'

Second young man: 'You ought to marry a teacher, then, or a nurse. They can always get work.'

A modern slant on the young man of the past who was looking for an heiress to marry!

Whenever we try to tie up with somebody else, there is the hope that they will provide something – money, security, status, beauty, youth – that we feel we lack ourselves. Nowadays, we form intimate partnerships out of deeply-felt need and inadequacy, not because we have to do so in order to survive, as in the past. It seems to me that the tightly-knit couple has had its day and is lingering on because we have not really learned new and better ways of relating to other people.

But if the hermetically-sealed, monogamous, lifelong couple is on its way out, what will be the replacement? Will there be lots of single, wholly individual people around in future, all loosely bonding and having close but detached relationships with each other, all connecting to their community and the wider world, having a sense of purpose and personal fulfilment which does not depend on a particular relationship to another person?

I certainly sincerely hope so. Looser bonds make for healthier relationships and better friendships all round. But how is this to be achieved? Clearly, we can't go back, we can only go forward.

Several social anthropologists have made the point that the nuclear family is actually about the most unhealthy unit there is. It elevates men at the expense of women, isolates and imprisons women in their homes and makes for a wasteful society, where each of us has to have our own washing machine, spin drier, dishwasher, car and so on. And although we may all long for these things and see them as labour-saving and modern, the fact is that there are simply not enough resources in the world for every single nuclear family to have its suburban-type home with garden, garage, car, lawnmower and two holidays a year.

Nuclear families create extremes of rich and poor, and the feeling that the family must be protected and preserved at any cost, even to the extent of forgetting that other people exist. Tightly-knit units can blind us to what is going on outside and make us feel completely unconnected with the rest of humanity.

Some people believe that the answer may be to live in communities, or communes, and share everything more, have co-operatives and co-ownership. So far, these have had limited success, possibly because intimacy and bonding occur all too readily. True, there have been some successful communities in the past, but these are usually united by religious zeal or spiritual fervour. 'Secular' communities don't seem to be markedly successful.

I believe one reason why present-day communes have not been significantly successful is because of the overwhelming importance placed on having 'significant others' in our lives; we can't help but be touched and tainted by it. Also, communes will only ever work when there is a definite sense of purpose involved, when people do not band together just because they believe there will be a greater variety of sexual partners on offer, or because they imagine they will get free or very cheap accommodation, but when there is a common goal involved which is beneficial to everybody. I believe the ideal of the future is to live in larger communities, not to try and isolate ourselves in ever more secure houses with burglar alarms and intruder devices, but to try and come together, to trust each other more, to be able to love and let go and not to try to yoke somebody else to us in a kind of permanent thralldom.

Communities are, it seems to me, more 'natural' than nuclear families, more in accord with our deeper natures. The reason that little isolated families don't work is because they do not satisfy our deepest needs and yearnings, which are to connect to other people but to remain free inside our heads.

One of the few modern communities which does genuinely work and has done for over 30 years now, is that of Findhorn, in the north of Scotland. There, several hundred people, mainly single individuals, live and work in complete harmony. There is love, but not attachment, bonding, but not bondage. Of course, the humans there are not perfect people and problems do sometimes occur.

But because all have felt drawn to the place because of what it can give them and what they can give it, there is no feeling of loneliness or isolation, and, with the majority at least, no wish to bind together in exclusive units. If people started pairing off at a fast rate at Findhorn, the whole community would collapse. There could, it seems to me, be many more Findhorns in existence, if only we could lose our longing to be bound tightly to just one other person, and could use this energy to connect properly to other people, and work for the greater good, rather than just to feed and clothe our own little families. We would be enabled to see things globally, more clearly. As Bhagwan Shree Rajneesh said, there has never been, and never will be, a case of somebody embarking on a family after becoming enlightened. Once you start to think globally, once you become clear in your head, the desire to limit your horizons to trying to satisfy two or three other people, at most, will recede.

Whenever alternatives to the tightly-knit couple and the nuclear family are discussed, people always ask, thinking they have found the Achilles heel: but what about the children? Don't they need two parents, a loving, close home? Well, perhaps they do, but they rarely get it. It is estimated that around 92 per cent of American families are dysfunctional, by which is meant that each member is unable to be themselves, but is constrained into a role which limits and confuses them.

Thus the father may be defined as the 'breadwinner', the mother as the 'homemaker', and the children may be 'clever', 'pretty', 'the sporty one', and so on.

Everybody is defined and narrowed by the roles they play, or feel constrained to play, and nobody can be truly themselves. When we become part of an intimate couple, and even more when we become part of a family, we have to deny part of ourselves – the most important part, it seems to me, of what we truly are. We have to deny an aspect of our individuality, our uniqueness.

If we don't, we are often seen as not fulfilling our responsibilities. If we don't conform to what people expect of a spouse, a parent or a child, we are condemned for it. We all have to be the same.

But children don't have to be in tightly-sealed families to be happy; they can flourish in all kinds of situations, if they are genuinely loved and cared for – which is often not the case in the apparently closely-knit nuclear family. It is common for parents and teenagers not to be speaking, for grown-up children never to visit their aged parents, for children to be 'problems'. All this is accepted as normal – and so many people are deeply unhappy, coming from these apparently normal families.

Women feel guilty if they do go out to work, guilty if they don't. Men have affairs and feel guilty – nobody feels secure or genuinely loved, or has any real idea what they should be doing, how it can be made to work. The closely-tied couple, by its very nature, engenders guilt, which we then pass on to our children as something perfectly normal. We never had so many neuroses and emotionally troubled people before the nuclear family was held up as the norm for everybody.

Children can live happily with one parent, two or three; with aunts and grandmothers, with lesbian or gay parents, with a number of people bringing them up; there is nothing inherently secure or loving about having two parents of different sexes. In traditional extended families, children are in a sense shared, so there is not the same fierce attachment and possessiveness about them which we have in our very small units. There are not the same expectations and disappointments: not the same devastation if they don't pass exams, or let us down.

And anyway – we don't all have to have children. This is another thing that has happened as a result of the newly-close couple: we feel we have to seal the union, secure and define it with a new life. In the past, of course, it was common for a woman to get pregnant so that the man would marry her. Even now, it's not unknown for women to have children to keep their man, especially when the man in question is older, a bit of a rake, charismatic. There has been the idea that film star Warren Beatty, now in his fifties, will be 'tamed' and 'faithful' now that at last he is a father.

But what's so wonderful about being tamed, about being like everybody else? After all, there's nothing particularly clever in becoming a father; most men can do it without much effort.

Nowadays, because we all feel so isolated and unconnected, particularly to ourselves, we all feel we have to have our very own children. If you tell people with infertility problems who are trying to conceive that there are plenty of children already in existence, living in children's homes, who would love to join a loving family, they look at you oddly. They don't want one of *those* – it wouldn't be the same.

But again in traditional extended families, in a sense everybody did have children, or at least, had close and continuing contact with them, so there was not the same urge for everybody personally to reproduce. Now, we are not seen as complete unless we have not only the spouse, but the child as well. That means we're really successful, that we've really made it.

A home does not seem a proper home for long without the patter of tiny feet. Although at first, the relationship may seem to be enough, as the years go by and it gets boring, or starts to loosen, we feel the need to do something to liven it up, glue it together, make it more exciting. The only thing most people can come up with is to have a child, or perhaps two. It is no accident nowadays that a couple who have lived together for 10 or 12 years suddenly get married and have children – when it's all become routine and the fun has got tedious. Instead of trying to find a real sense of purpose in their lives, people are tying themselves down even more, in an attempt to give themselves a sense of greater permanence, greater security.

One of the reasons why the birthrate goes up and up in spite of ever more effective contraception is because we all now feel we have the 'right' to reproduce and 'find happiness' this way.

If being, and remaining single, were a more positive choice for people, this would lessen as well.

I have known so many people who, in their early and mid-twenties, swore they would never get married or have children. I meet them again in their forties or fifties, and what do I find: there's now a spouse and a couple of kids in tow. They've got mortgages, money problems, they're tired, they're tied – and they wonder why they're not happy. I have yet to see one formerly gloriously free person made happier and more 'fulfilled' by adding all these people to their lives, people who will not go away, at least until they are grown up.

People do it, they conform in the end because they lose courage, they get faint and weary, they start to feel there must be something wrong with them for being the only one in their crowd not to have the full kit, a partner of their own and also a little family.

There is at the moment no encouragement to stay single, to be your own person. It is seen as selfish, non-life-affirming. Decisions to remain unhooked are not, on the whole, respected. They are viewed as eccentric, minority.

People keep saying to me: 'You'll feel differently when you meet somebody,' wanting to put me in the same position as themselves. They feel, or want to feel, that I am 'protesting too much' and making the best of a bad job when I maintain that I am happier being on my own, and fully intend to stay that way.

The main message I want to put over with this book is to

reassure people that singleness does not mean loneliness or isolation – far from it. It is the couple, not singleness, that is isolating and alienating. In couples, it can be hard to connect properly to other people and the world at large. When we are alone, we can have the freedom to do this. It's not necessary for every single one of us to found our very own tiny little dynasty, either for our own happiness or security or for the sake of the world. In fact, the fewer people we have coming into the world, all with personality and relationship and learning problems, the better for humanity in general.

Being single is not lonely, it is not boring and it is not frightening. There is a greater sense of personal security when we acknowledge that we can rely on nobody but ourselves, in the end, and that nobody can give or remove our happiness, than when we imagine we can gain this by intimate alliances.

Being single does not mean you have to try to be an island, entire unto yourself. It means you have reclaimed yourself, that you have the courage to live how you want to live, unhampered by the wishes of an intimate other, and that you have the freedom to find and develop a sense of purpose, your talents, your true individuality. You won't go mad, you'll go sane.

You're not missing out, you're gaining.

# Further Reading

Allen, Yvonne: *Successfully Single*. Heinemann, 1987.

Chester, Carole: *Going Alone: The Woman's Guide to Travel Know-How*. Helm, 1987.

Dowling, Colette: *The Cinderella Complex: Women's Hidden Fear of Independence*. Fontana, 1982.

Eichenbaum, Luise and Orbach, Susie: *What do Women Want?* Fontana, 1984.

Formaini, Heather: *Men: The Darker Continent*. Heinemann, 1990.

Franks, Helen: *Remarriage*. Bodley Head, 1988.

Honey, Peter: *Solving Your Personal Problems*. Sheldon Press, 1987.

Jeffers, Susan: *Dare To Connect*. Piatkus, 1992.

Jeffreys, Sheila: *The Spinster and Her Enemies: Feminism and Sexuality 1880-1930*. Pandora, 1985.

Kahn, Sandra S: *The Ex-Wife Syndrome*. Ebury, 1991.

Kingma, Daphne Rose: *Coming Apart. Why Relationships End, and How to Live Through the Ending of Yours*. Conari Press, 1987.

Lynch, James: *The Broken Heart: The Medical Consequences of Loneliness*. Basic Books, New York, 1977.

Marlow, Mary Elizabeth: *Handbook for the Emerging Woman*. The Donning Company, Virginia Beach, 1988.

Peiffer, Vera: *Positively Single*. Element, 1991.

Rajneesh, Bhagwan Shree: *A New View of Women's Liberation*. The Rebel Publishing House GmbH, West Germany, 1987.

Raymond, Janice: *A Passion for Friends*. The Women's Press, 1986.

Rodwell, Lee: *The Single Woman's Survival Guide*. Thorsons, 1985.

Simenauer J. and Carroll, D: *Singles: The New Americans*. Simon and Schuster, 1982.

Storr, Anthony: *Solitude*. Flamingo, 1989.

Taylor, Liz McNeill: *Living Alone: A Woman's Guide*. Sheldon, 1987.

Underwood, Lynn: *One's Company: A Practical Guide to Enjoying Your Independence*. Ashford, Southampton, 1989.

Wallerstein, Judith S: *Second Chances: Men, Women and Children A Decade After Divorce*. Transworld, 1989.

Wilson, Mary: *Suddenly Single*. Columbus, 1985.